Once Upon Cape Cod
From
Cockle Cove to the Powder Hole

A Book Of Essays
By
Dana Eldridge

Foreword by John A. Ullman

Cover illustration by Douglas W. Turner

Other illustrations by Robert La Pointe

Stony Brook Publishing & Productions, Inc.
Brewster, Ma.

Published by Stony Brook Publishing & Productions, Inc.
25 Stony Hill Road
Brewster, MA 02631
(508-896-2514)

Cover design and page layout by Joe Gallante
Stony Brook Publishing & Productions, Inc.

For ordering information, contact the author at
Post Office Box 576
East Orleans, MA 02643

To Lynne

Contents

Part I

Part II

Acknowledgments

There is no way to thank all the people who have helped along the way, and so I gratefully acknowledge the following: my folks, who made it easy to fall in love with literature and also passed on their love of the Cape; David Manual and John Ullman, who encouraged me to *get it on paper*; Greg O'Brien, who is a superb editor and has become a good friend—without his good counsel this book probably would not have seen the light of day.

But most of all, to the most patient, loving friend this man could have—my wife, Lynne.

Foreword

This is a love story.

Perhaps several love stories. It covers a large part of the life of a man born and brought up in the lap of luxury.

His parents had little money. His grandparents had little money. His neighbors had little money. But they all had Chatham. And having Chatham, they had Cape Cod, the Atlantic, the beaches, the ponds, the piney woods, and all the wealth of good things that were there.

Dana Eldridge, who gives us this glimpse into his love life is more than a good writer. He is, to our lasting benefit, a storyteller.

In the telling, he gives us—in almost a stream of consciousness style—wonderful essays about the early days of Chatham where he grew up, and even something of the Chatham that is there now and astonishingly little changed.

The luxury to which he was born was a cornucopia that debouched all the oysters one could eat, all the little necks one could want, all the snapper blues one could consume, and all the salty out-of-doors one could inhale.

His childhood in Chatham and on Chatham's Monomoy Island was the place that formed his character; and Dana knows it. And so he reaches into his memory and brings forth, as immediate as the weather today, what life and living was like where everything a boy or young man could dream of was all around him, waiting to be consumed.

A writer would have polished the material. Dana simply tells it, and it lives.

His boat leaks. His gas tank got along on a gallon of gas or 50 cents worth, whichever was available. His parents loved him and punished him. His grandfather loved him and taught him to fish, or to find the best place for soft shell clams.

Today, men and women, and even children, come by their hundreds of thousands and their traffic punishing miles to experience for a week or two what Dana Eldridge had when he stepped out the door.

Growing up in Chatham in the 30's when drinking water came from the kitchen pump, and left through the nearby privy, changed to Chatham in the 40's when things were scarce on the war-time shelves, but of unlimited availability on the Chatham shores.

This book jumps around a little—from a young man sailing a leaky catboat, to a 10-year-old stuck up to the neck in a mudhole in a swamp, to a teenager riding with his grandfather who drives by impulse, to a 10-year-old falling out of a pine tree, clutching baby crows to his chest.

Like all love stories, this is a ride for the willing and appreciative venturesome. It has it ups and downs, and a good many sideways.

But it will live on the bookshelves to be brought out to prove a point, or win a bet, or while away a rainy day.

We can't review it without telling it, and Dana tells it better. Enjoy.

John A. Ullman
Eastham, Massachusetts

Once Upon Cape Cod

From

Cape Cod

Cockle Cove to the Powder Hole

Part I

Chatham

C hatham, pronounced *"Chatum,"* is at the elbow of Cape Cod. It is not on the way to anywhere. That's one of its many charms. For its size, Chatham probably has more miles of waterfront than any other town on the Cape. Indeed, it is all but surrounded by water—nearly all of it salt, and nearly all of it protected from the open ocean.

Chatham also boasts a ten-mile long sandy finger that points southwest towards Nantucket, just over the horizon. This thin strip of sand cannot decide whether it wants to be an island or a peninsula, so it tries each guise from time to time. But whatever the mood, it is jewel-like in its beauty and munificent in its bounty. Its name, a relic of the natives that preceded us on this land, is Monomoy.

At the easterly flank of this eastmost Cape town is another sandy peninsula, North Beach, which originates in Orleans ten miles north. The vicissitudes of the winds and tides rearrange these sandy outposts at will and always in a generally north-south direction.

Chatham is still riven with salt ponds and rivers, and shares with surrounding towns a large portion of a beautiful body of water, Pleasant Bay, formerly Monomoyick Bay. A sizable segment of the town's population has always turned to these rich surrounding waters for their sustenance, and many still do.

Nature bestowed her blessings with a heavy hand when she designed this town. It is indeed a coy beauty, often peeking out from under a blanket of moisture. It has been said that Chatham makes fog for the rest of the nation, and maybe it does. Certainly the confluence of that ice cold water and the warm air constitute the makings of a fog factory. And nature doesn't disappoint. Fog is a fact of life on the Cape's elbow. It makes the gardens grow with vigor, causes mariners nervous moments, but is not unpleasant to experience in short doses. It usually dissipates by mid-morning.

The Chatham of the 1930, 40s and 50s was a very rural place. Our home was in the furthest corner of town, right against the Harwich border, as far west on Nantucket Sound as is possible to go and still be in Chatham.

Every summer, the year-round house was rented out, and we moved to remote Eel Pond River, to a 12 by 12 foot cottage (a former hen house) with a tiny bunk room. It was the only dwelling on nearly one hundred acres of family land. We had a privy with a magnificent view of the winding river and the beaches beyond. There was no electricity in the cottage. Every other day ice pickup at the local ice plant was the only bow towards refrigeration. The cottage was so small that I was relegated to private digs out in the woods, an 8 by 10 foot wall tent. There wasn't even a road into this bucolic site. We had to wend our way through the pitch pines.

There were some real benefits in living out by the river—acres of woods and miles of dirt roads to explore, ponds to swim in, rivers to row. It was like a gigantic present just waiting to be explored by young eyes. Civilization had not had its constricting way with the land in that era. But few of us appreciated this gift until our own children came along, and the boundaries were much closer.

Growing up in this remote part of a small town where everyone knew everyone was like growing up in a large family. There were the petty annoyances, but also a safe and comfortable feeling that everyone cared. In South Chatham where about a quarter of the residents were related in some way, this comfortable feeling was wonderfully exaggerated.

Chatham must have been a land of milk and honey for its early inhabitants—ample game in the woods, plentiful fish and shellfish in the shallow waters, fresh water pouring out of the ground, and a benign climate year-round. For the generations of Native Americans that called this place home, life must have been easy and rewarding.

That all changed when a feisty (probably cantankerous, certainly adventurous) weaver named William Nickerson, my earliest direct ancestor in the New World, arrived from Norwich, England in the 1600s. He had decided the recently created town of Boston was too crowded for him, so he hitched up his ox team, gathered up his family and headed east to the largely unexplored lands of Cape Cod. His internal compass must have been fixated on east because he stopped only when he could no longer go in that direction, settling in a land called by its few Native American inhabitants, Monomoyick. He liked the lay of this land (how could he not), and like all Europeans, wanted to possess it. He negotiated with the local sachem for the purchase of what is now the northeast corner of town.

Bureaucracy, however, was not to be denied. As soon as the Crown Colony got wind of this transaction, they sent a minion to inform this doughty settler that nobody negotiated with the Indians, nobody except the Crown Colony itself. His purchase was deemed invalid, and he was fined 200 pounds sterling for violating the strictures of the Crown. William Nickerson wasn't about to pay any fine for the privilege of having the Crown act as a real estate agent for land he had already purchased. Rather, he ignored the Crown and hied himself and his growing family to remote regions in the hopes the fracas would blow over in time. When he returned 10 years later, he negotiated with the same sachem for the additional purchase of about three thousand more acres of the Cape's finest land. The Crown huffed and puffed, threatened dire punishments, but this rugged settler utterly ignored them.

My grandfather, William Sears Nickerson, in his delightful essay, *The Bay—As I See It*, wrote of the old settler buying Chatham.

> "From my front door I can also see the hills over across the Bay under the lee of which my immigrant ancestor built his pioneer cabin," he wrote. "William Nickerson was the first white man to settle in the Land of the Monomoyicks. His house stood at the head of Ryder's Cove in Chathamport next door to the wigwam of the Old Sagamore from whom he had bought his land. Here they grew old together, the white man and the red, good neighbors always. It is here that he and the old Sagamore from whom he bought his land by fair and open bargain sleep in eternal peace"

> "For the decade covering King Phillips War scarcely another settler dared the dangers of this frontier outpost. The old pioneer ruled his domain like a patriarch, dispensing justice and teaching religion with almost utter disregard for the civil and spiritual authorities of the Colony."

Old William had twelve surviving children. The eldest daughter married a released indentured servant from Yarmouth named Robert Eldred, thus starting the first intermingling of Nickerson-Eldridge bloodlines. Twelve generations later my father, Wib, a

Chatham Eldridge, married a lissome Harwich girl, Elizabeth Nickerson—as Cape Cod a couple as anyone could devise. The Eldridges, it should be noted, come in two flavors: the *"i"* Eldridges, and the *"e"* Eldredges. One of the many stories about the varied spelling is that the *"i"* Eldridges were horse thieves and the *"e"* Eldredges would steal anything. We belonged to the *"i"* Eldridges, and there weren't many horses in town.

My parents had a soul-deep love of the land and all that it could produce—a love they passed down to their children and their grandchildren. They enjoyed life to the fullest. They had a bountiful garden and harvested all manner of fish and shellfish from the waters around them. My parents were frugal by necessity, but somehow they made it fun. There were trips to the shore for the adventure of getting enough clams for dinner, spring trips to the herring run for a few dozen fish for baked herring or a meal of red roes, and many oystering expeditions.

Over the years, we had an assortment of tired craft. The jewel of the assortment was a 17-foot catboat. Catboats are a particularly Cape Cod boat, very likely developed right here by long shore fishermen who wanted a simply-rigged fast boat that would carry a good load. *"She turns quick as a cat."* Hence the term, catboat. Our old catboat was decidedly limber. On the mooring, she did fine, but once the sail was bent on and hoisted, the strains of that bow-mounted mast started to wrack the weary hull, and most of Nantucket Sound came through for a visit. *That* boat had clean bilges. Our weekend sails were accompanied by noisy laughter and vigorous splashings, as the old wooden bailer was put to work restoring the sound to its rightful place. Over the years, this old catboat and numerous sharpies (one aptly named "Inertia") were pressed into service in the warmer months to take us to the clam flats of Monomoy, or out on Nantucket Sound for an afternoon of bailing and sailing with the playful dolphins. We almost always had a shiny lure towing along behind, just in case a bluefish wanted to join us for dinner.

My parents did most everything together. One activity that still amazes people is the fact that my mother used to enjoy duck hunting (and still would if she could). On the good duck days, those cold, gray, blustery winter days, she and my dad would get up before dawn, get all swathed in layers of tan canvas, don their boots, gather their guns and a few shells, and head for the East or West Meadows to garner a few black ducks or a goose for dinner. They were often successful. Success meant a flurry of duck feathers or a mountain of goose feathers out back of the barn. It also meant a dark brown, savory, steaming fowl on the table with—if time allowed—oyster stuffing oozing out of the cracks and crevices. It was rich and rewarding eating.

"Use it up!" "Make do!" These were the watchwords of the Depression years, and my folks lived by them. Mother even made her own laundry soap through some alchemy with animal fats and other unknown substances. The remnants of used soap bars were gathered and held in a wooden-handled wire device that allowed the user to swish it around in dishwater to extract the last sud from the often unyielding soap bar.

The Depression was in full swing when I came along in 1931. Recycling and saving was a way of life. But the soul-withering effects of the Great Depression was something that happened on the other side of the bridge. This bountiful land, our Cape, made (and still makes) food getting easy and fun.

Most Cape Codders were not greatly affected by the stock market crash. Most of us were poor to begin with, and food was readily available at the end of any road, on the flats, or at sea. All one needed was a bucket, a scratcher (one of those multi-tined long toothed rakes), a clam hoe, and a low tide. Clams, those succulent steamer clams, were there for the digging, and quohogs lay just under the surface of the obliging flats. The old wooden jetty with its stone rip rap was just one place one could expect to find oysters. The end of the road was a storehouse of shellfish of any kind. Easy pickings.

My folks' sense of responsibility was well-developed, and like most first-time young parents, they were far more nervous about my survival than they probably needed to be. My mother, upon looking back on her 60 years as a parent, recently allowed that she had worried too much and mostly about the wrong things—probably the lament of any parent, although mother was, and is, a world-class worrier.

Wib, my dad, would best be described as a stolid man with a decidedly stubborn streak, qualities that stood him in good stead all his life. He had a dry sense of humor and a ready grin. Both my sister and I called him *Wib*, as did every one else in town. It never occurred to us to call him *Dad*, and apparently he never wanted us to. *Wib* was our equivalent of Dad.

Wib was steady. Whatever came along, he stayed the course, a perfect attribute for his life in the banking business. He also was an avid waterman when he could find the time and a great gardener. His gardens were the talk of the town. From what looked like sterile sand, up would spring luxuriant crops of vegetables.

My relationship with Wib was sometimes distant, but mostly I remember the good times we had together. Wib was of an era when kids were supposed to be seen and not heard. I was both seen and heard.

Mother was the energizer of the family. She worked hard, and she played hard. Her enjoyment of good books, her love of the beaches, of her heritage, of the Cape itself, were attributes my sister and I have inherited in abundance. She ran the smallest library in the state for 40 some years, and passed on her love of good books to the town's youngsters, myself included. Being a very small library in South Chatham, open only three hours a week, meant new books were delivered to the house, which, in turn, meant that I had first crack at reading them. This was a gift of rare circumstance, and one that was appreciated wholeheartedly.

If ever there was a bona fide Cape Codder, mother was it. Her love of her land was only eclipsed by her love of her soul mate, Wib. Their bond was all encompassing, much tighter than any boat they ever owned.

When I was 13 my only sibling, Beth, was born. She was and still is a presence. She has a ready laugh, and a bone-deep love for the Cape and all its bounty. From our father, she inherited an appreciation of the soil and all it can produce. Her gardens are well organized and abundantly prolific. Beth also has laser vision when it comes to clams. If there are any around, she will find them and have them in a pot shortly thereafter. She is also a joy to know, and adds to her luster by being a gourmet cook.

Extended Family

Looking back, there seemed to be little disdain between generations. We all welcomed the rare times when the older generations joined in the fun. The extended family played a big part in our lives. Uncles, aunts, and cousins dotted the landscape; I felt a part of an enormous whole. Every Thanksgiving and every Christmas we all gathered at my grandparents' home to renew the family bonds. These were happy times; petty concerns were put on the shelf. A palpable feeling of happiness enshrouded the growing families in an aura of joy, as we all pulled our chairs up to the groaning and laden table. The bronzed, steaming turkey, the white mounds of hot mashed potatoes, squashes, carrots, gravy boats full of viscous, and savory gravy, were all part of the glue that makes a festive family feast work. Desserts were rich and plentiful. The pecan pies, the apple pies, buckets of white, fluffy whipped cream, and platters of hard sauce, were all made in the kitchen on the old wood stove.

On the morning of this bacchanal, Grandpa Eldridge and I would go to the nearest cranberry bog with an ax and a burlap bag in hand to gather some ice. Then it was back to the house to make some ice cream with the old hand-cranked machine, a morning project that was all work and all fun. The grinding, cranking, slushy mix of ice and rock salt slowly melting as it gradually gave up its cold to the thickening mix in the revolving steel canister is the stuff of rich memories. The handle turned harder and harder, as the mix turned from thin sweet soup to thick sweet ice cream. At the right time, judged by Grandpa as the resident ice cream expert, the cranking stopped, the mixing paddle was withdrawn, and most of the frozen mix was scraped back into the container. But not all. Some of this delicious ice cold sweetness was removed by the cranker, as one would demolish an ice cream cone by dint of some inspired slurping. It was the reward for the patient cranking to make the stuff, and also a promise for future cranking exercises.

The entire Eldridge family was located within a three mile radius, easily within walking distance. Their homes were a place to go to talk with someone that *understood* without explanation, a place to go when parental restrictions weighed heavily.

My Eldridge grandparents lived a half-mile distant. In this sprawling home also lived my grandfather's mother and my grandmother's father and mother. The word grandparent is just right, for they were grand parents, who offered all of the love and succor, with none of the discipline; all of the delicious goodies, with none of the admonitions. It was an altogether choice arrangement, and one I made the most of for years. The brown scotch-taped cracks in the top of Nana Eldridge's green cookie jar are as vivid in memory today as they were in reality then. The jar was always full and I was so lucky. As I was the first grandchild for a decade or so, love and attention was lavished on me in abundance.

Grampa Eldridge was an ideal grandfather, a role model for all grandparents. According to family lore, he was not too interested in small babies, but once these bits of humanity got their "heads screwed on," his interest and love was deep and abiding. Physically, Grampa wasn't anything remarkable—a short, mildly overweight man, with an easy grin, and a gait that rolled slightly when he walked. This habit came not from striding the decks of a pitching vessel, but rather from his rather unusual job of working the mail train. He worked for the railroad—one week on, one week off. That schedule left plenty of time for teaching his first, grandchild the rudiments of life on the Cape. I was an apt student.

Grampa was there when it was time to learn fishing techniques for the snapper blues, flounder, and stripers from the surf. My first memories of this man's fishing involved being on the east side of Monomoy, watching him "heaving and hauling" for stripers. There was no pole, just a long tarred line arrayed on the beach in such a manner as to make the heave tangle free. The line with a heavy lure (drail) attached was swung around a few times to build up momentum, and then released. The retrieve was hand-over-hand. The line arrayed on the beach tangle free for the next heave. The heaving and hauling was hard work, and it took a lot of room on the beach. For these reasons, Grampa bought one of the first salt water casting poles in town, a Calcutta cane bamboo pole that served him well for many years.

Grampa was always ready to try something new. Years before he had purchased one of the first horseless carriages in town—a Hudson that was steered by a tiller and was so under powered that it had to be backed up long hills.

In today's parlance, Grampa would be called "laid back." At the time, it was just *easy going*. For example, he taught me to drive (this was long before the days of drivers' ed), though he took driving very casually himself. He was not above taking off his own garage doors now and again by forgetting to open them when he backed out, or running over whatever was lying around the yard because he hadn't bothered to see what was behind him.

When Grampa and his big Buick loomed into sight, those of us who knew of his driving habits gave him a wide berth, and those that didn't soon learned to beware. In teaching me to drive, his admonitions were gentle and delivered with no sting. The "lessons" were a bit surreal. On the way to the Harding's Beach dirt parking lot where he had me practice my maneuvers, he would ask my advice about whether the car ahead of us was driving towards us or away from us. He was all but blind.

But what I remember most about this man was his kindness to me and to those around him. In showing me the rudiments of fishing, he deliberately let me catch more than he did. He let me be the "hi-liner" without my ever knowing he was doing so. I never was able to thank him, other than to delight in his company. Thank you, Grampa.

Grampa died suddenly from complications following routine surgery. He was only 69, and I was still a teenager. Death is the final act in life; when it comes on the scene, only memories are left. For me the memories are bright, rich, and soul satisfying. I felt like hell when the phone rang and Nana Eldridge told us Grampa had died. It didn't seem right. Until then I had thought the good times would go on forever. What did he mean leaving me like that? How was I supposed to cope with that often uncertain world without his help? That first night I tried to envision some scenario whereby the phone would ring and we would be told that it was all a mistake, that someone who *looked* like Grampa had died. Of course, that didn't happen, but oh how I wanted it to be.

Now that my own grand parenting days are here, I remember the wonderful, warm, safe, feelings engendered by my own experiences with my uncritical grandparents, and I try to emulate their love and many kindnesses.

Our Little Group

South Chatham's children were scant on the ground. There were just a few other kids near my age, and one of them was biologically a girl. But she "outboyed" us in every way. She was heavily built and a terror with the boxing gloves (she hit with an open handed slap—being raked by those laces really hurt), and she was a true competitor in every childhood game. We boys were taught to be gentle with the girls, but that didn't work with Cassie. She didn't do gentle, and because she didn't, we boys took our lumps.

She was good fun, though, and game for anything. I remember the time she was holding on to a dock while standing in a rowboat. As the gap between the dock and the boat slowly got wider and wider, immersion was imminent. Her wails were nothing compared to our laughter. The splash when it came was mighty, and in our little group—at least for the moment—the mighty had fallen. I can still see the sailor's cap she always wore bobbing away on the ebbing tide. I can also see the grim set to her jaw, as she emerged from her impromptu bath and started up the path toward us—a look she apparently was practicing for her years as shellfish warden in the town of Chatham.

My friend Warren was quiet. He lived down the street in the only "unelectrified" house in town, a house with a privy out back and a hand pump just outside the backdoor. The privy and pump did land office business in 1938 and 1944 when hurricanes came barreling through and the town had no electricity to pump water for more than a week. Warren, too, was game for any of our schemes, and we had many adventures together in the woods, marshes and waters of our little town. His life was even more frugal than mine, but not by much. His dad had no car. Instead, he rode a bike wherever he wanted to go—this in an era when anyone over 25 was considered by us twerps to be over the hill. Riding bikes was, in our minds, something reserved for the young.

Just next door to Warren were fairly recent imports to town, a family of transplanted New Jerseyites. The family included a boy named Bo who was about our age and he fit right in, particularly after a leavening process of competitive daring do—races, fights, the usual rough and tumble of young life. Bo was not as easy going as Warren, but we usually got along just fine. His round face, so like a younger version of his father's, would break into a toothy grin at the slightest provocation.

For a short period, the three of us couldn't get along, and so Bo and I divided the amenable Warren. He got Warren on Mondays,

Wednesdays and Fridays, and I played with Warren on alternate days. At the time it seemed like a logical solution to the squabbles we'd been having. It was logical enough. It just didn't work for long.

There were two other kids in town, about five years older. When they needed pawns, they put us to work, particularly if the work was dangerous. One of the older kids, Jack, was a budding chemist, who was able to buy explosives, even during World War II. We younger, expendable types mixed all manner of volatile house-flattening mixes in his parents' basement. I noticed that when we were asked to slowly stir and dry some gray "goo" under a heat lamp, Jack stayed outside. Some evidence of one of Jack's explosive schemes still exists in Red River beside Deep Hole Road on the Chatham-Harwich line. A flattened concrete culvert end is still in the river where two ounces of methyl nitrate put it fifty years ago. Everyone in town knew who was behind the mysterious explosions. Chatham's sole policeman paid a call on Jack.

"I know you are the one blowing up the culverts," he said. *"If I ever catch you, I'll send you to jail."*

It didn't deter Jack at all. He continued his explosive ways.

And that is the sum total of kids in our small corner of the town who were near our age. When I was 15 or so, another new family moved into town, a family with two beautiful girls and three boys all about our age. This new family stimulated the activities of us few kids, and probably the whole town for months. They were *everything* we were not. They were Catholic when everyone else in town was not; they were Democrats when everyone else in town was not; they seemed to have no visible means of support, while everyone's father worked. They were practically aliens, and for awhile were viewed as such.

Even though we didn't see it at the time, the Cape was changing right before our eyes. Newcomers with new ways were moving in and we would have to make way for them. These newcomers soon became so commonplace that the fact that they were Democrats, or Catholics, or from New Jersey was no longer noteworthy. These off-breeds that we had been hearing about in the most dire terms turned out to be just like us. They worried about the same things, played the same games, and their girls were certainly the prettiest we had ever encountered.

The leavening occurred in both cultures, the new and the old. What had been a mostly very *like-thinking* group of kids was now stirred up, homogenized, mixed with others from distant parts. It was the best thing that could have happened to us, though we were slow to realize it. Insular people tend to isolate themselves, tend to resist anything new. Our generation resisted for a short while, but the very dearth of children in the neighborhood made the assimilation that much easier. Those two beautiful girls didn't hurt the mixing process, either.

One great benefit of living in a resort community was the seasonal infusion of new blood. At least half of the summer population were visitors. Every summer, families came from inland to share our pristine beaches and inviting waters. It was common in those days to have families move here for the entire summer. Usually, the father would commute to work and come back weekends. Mother and children would stay for the summer. Our summertime next door neighbors did this every year. When Pierce Massey came back for the weekend—if the tide was low enough to wade Red River—he would leave the bus in Harwichport and walk the three miles of Nantucket Sound beach to his beach front cottage. It was a pleasant enough walk. It must have seemed a welcome contrast to the hustle and bustle of New York City, his workplace. I've often wondered what beachgoers he encountered along the way made of this pin-striped, dark suited character—his Homburg neatly in place, his briefcase in one hand, his shoes and socks in the other— striding along the white sands of those beautiful beaches.

This man taught me the value of just being on the beach. Until I met Pierce, beaches had been something on the way to getting fish or shellfish. Pierce delighted in just being on the edge of the continent with fish pole in hand and his bare feet in the surf. He apparently had little interest in the fish. I saw him walk away from easily caught, breaking fish, just casting into the calm waters and enjoying himself to the utmost. Being there was his goal, not that he spurned any fish that blundered into his lure. Indeed, he was quite proud of a scar on one of his fingers, a scar made by a ferocious 15-pound bluefish that clamped onto his finger with the force of lockgrip pliers. When Pierce, in justifiable alarm and pain, hurriedly retrieved his hand, the back of one finger was laid open to the bone. The bite left a wonderful and obvious scar, and forever after, the catalyst for the retelling.

"What's that terrible scar on your finger, Pierce?"

"Did I ever tell you about the big bluefish I caught on Monomoy."

Pierce would be off, recounting the wonderful day on the beach when he was attacked by an angry fish. Over time a few embellishments were added to flavor the story.

The Masseys were good, solid friends for all the summers we lived side-by-side. These long stays by the summer people formed long-lasting friendships between the locals and washashores. About the time we were tired of the same old winter faces, a new crop of summer faces arrived on the scene. The excitement of new and renewed relationships would enliven our lives. And about the time these new faces began to wear thin, they would vanish and we would renew our friendships with the year-round gang.

It was a good arrangement, one that provided us with continuity and change all at once. It made it easier for us to get used to the changes that were sweeping and altering the face and flavor of the Cape.◆

Another Cape Cod

South Chatham was a wonderful place to live, and still is. There were always fish in the streams, animals and birds in the woods, and shellfish for the taking on the flats. There were fields, woods, beaches, marshes, and cranberry bogs to explore. It was a giant playground, and we used it to our utmost.

I remember one day a friend and I were walking on the flats. We were way out from the beach, at least half a mile from the nearest person. It was a typical beautiful summer day, not a cloud in the sky. The shoal water was full of promise. There were crabs to bedevil, tiny fish to chase, jellyfish to marvel at, and a myriad of unknown mysterious things to experience, things with a slight aura of the sinister for a six-year-old explorer—all good stuff, this thin Nantucket soup.

We were alone on the edge of our universe. Well, almost alone. Way across the flats were two fawn-colored, horse-sized animals that were coming our way. The wavering distortion of distance made their actual shapes unclear. Were they fanged lions or thundering buffaloes? We weren't sure, but we could see enough to know that *whatever* they were, they were big, and they were coming our way.

Imagination and uncertainty, it was a sure recipe for terror. We fed mightily off each other's fears. We had no options for escape, and those two huge fearsome unknowns were still coming. It was pretty obvious that they could easily outrun us. To the north and south, the flats went on for miles. To the east, the nearest tree to climb was in Portugal, an ocean away. And to the west were those approaching, menacing shapes. We backed waist-deep into the water, and awaited our fate.

Whatever they were, they were now galloping. They looked like gigantic dogs, as tall as we were.

And that's just what they proved to be, just a pair of friendly, lolling-tongued Great Danes—a breed we had heard about but had never seen. They were coming over to play with the only other two living creatures on those featureless flats. They had seen us as potential playmates. We had seen them as hungry, boy-eating monsters. Perception is the putty of the mind. The Cape can be a scary place on the way up the large hill of experience.

Going For Snapper Blues

Like me, Grampa Eldridge also liked to have his feet in the salt water. His doings were always equated with fun.

"Do you want to go bluefishing?" he asked one day.

I'd never been before, but it didn't take any convincing. I was always ready for whatever Grampa wanted to do.

One of the delightful rites of passage for a young Cape Codder is learning to fish. At a very early age, my grandfather introduced me to snapper blues. Snapper blues are easy to catch, require a bare minimum of costly equipment, and if you land one, you will in all likelihood catch all you need. Snapper blues are easy to prepare and so very good to eat—a near perfect fish.

The first project of this expedition was to get the poles ready. These were 10-to-12-foot long, light bamboo poles somewhere near straight. A little crooked didn't matter much. The poles were retrieved from the dusty garage rafters. Line and hooks were replaced as needed. There was no reel; the line was wound around the pole

The second project, as much fun as the fishing itself, was getting the bait. The sacrificial victims, silversides, were netted from the nearby shallows. This involved a 10-foot seine, two people, a bucket, and a very small amount of expertise. The small seine (U-shaped) was slowly worked along the shore and carefully brought up on a shelving beach. The fun part was checking out the catch: seaweed (gobs of it), half a dozen small crabs, occasionally a fast-moving, finger-crunching blue crab, many mummichogs, a few baby flounders, and—if the sweep went well—a slew of silversides. All but the silversides were released to pursue their watery ways.

Fishing was the third project, the delightful climax to the buildup and anticipation. Jacknife Harbor was high on Grampa's short list of snapper blue hot spots. All the ingredients were there—the deep water right next to shore and a nice little eddy to keep the bait out in the stream where the snapper's lurked. Best of all, from Grampa's point of view, this particular spot was adjacent to a dirt road. Grampa wasn't much of a walker.

We always tried to get there on the rising tide. Snappers and most other fish bite best with the tide surging around them, swirling and riling the bait in helpless confusion.

The poles would come out of the car, and the cork checked to see if it was the proscribed foot-and-a-half from the hook. Then it was just a matter of attaching the hapless silversides to the hook, dropping the rig in the water, and waiting. If the fish were there, and they usually were, the cork would start its little dance. *Twitch, twitch, yank,* and under it went. That was the signal for us to give a twitch of the rod ourselves and deposit a furious little bluefish on the marsh bank. The contests Grampa and I used to have are happily seared in my memory: who could get the most, who would be the highliner, who was the better fisherman? Looking back on it, I'm sure he used to fish with a bare hook half the time, letting me "beat" him, allowing me to work my way up life's ladder with a little boost now and then, an almost unconscious training each generation passes on to the next.

Today we fish for these little fighters with graphite rods, sophisticated reels, nylon lines, artificial lures, and we often go after them with boats. It somehow seems absurd — a $10,000 boat, rods and reels worth hundreds of dollars, all for a few six-ounce fish. Maybe we have lost sight of the source of the pleasure. It often seems when we streamline a process, we whittle away some of the essence. It never was just the fish, it was the whole experience — the preparations, the seining, the fishing, and the eating. Mostly, it was the time spent with Grampa, and in a small way providing for the family. As fun as it was, fishing was a precursor to adulthood. I can clearly remember the small feeling of pride, knowing that I had caught and cleaned the evening meal. Free, delicious food.

The Cottage On Eel Pond River

One way my family supplemented its income, as I noted earlier, was by renting out the year-round house on Pleasant Street. This was an annual routine, and an eagerly awaited one. We always moved close to salt water. The first such move was to a tiny cottage (we called it a camp) on the Eel Pond River.

The setting was magnificent—30 feet above a tidal river with a near view of the winding creek, and *over* the water-veined marshes, a far view of Nantucket Sound and its beaches. Across the blue waters of the sound, a thin, strand of white stretched along the horizon, Monomoy.

The little creek was full of life—clams, oysters, quahogs year-round, and bass, bluefish, blue crabs, and flounders in season. You could wade in at low tide, and swim it at high tide. It was a safe place for a kid to learn to use a boat, to learn to swim, to learn about life. I was an apt and persistent student.

One life lesson was learning to calm my vivid imagination. Fear and darkness are ancient handmaidens, and for a 10-year-old can assume gargantuan proportions. I thought I was once in the clutches of a homicidal maniac bent on dismembering me bit by bit, but only after slowly strangling me in my tent. The delicate touch came out of the darkness, the feather-light fingertips searching my face for my vulnerable throat. There was no sound, just those searching, stealthy, threatening caresses, lightly over my forehead, down my face, across my lips and over my chin going for the throat. With a bellow that should have registered on a seismograph, I jumped out the cot and into the woods, the flashlight slicing away at the darkness, like Excaliber. My opponent was my imagination. The "villain" was a curious and totally harmless "Daddy-Long-Legs" spider, a very startled one at that.

Clamming At Cockle Cove

Coming of age in this tiny community was a warm, and at the same time, exciting process. My folks, like most of the other people in town, were of generations of Cape stock, well versed in making do and well used to living from the land. Since I was their first child—and for most of my childhood their only child—we had lots of experiences together, some with inconclusive results on both sides. And like good experimenters, we kept trying to get it *right*. We had lots of adventures and often in unlikely places

"Why do you always get into such scrapes?" they would ask. *"Every time we leave you alone you get into something. Now dammit, you're grounded. You are not to go out of sight of this camp for the next two weeks."*

This was only the latest in a string of edicts passed down as my parents tried to cope with child rearing. It was an ongoing contest between us. This occasion was, from a 10-year-old boy's point of view, not much to carry on about. From my inexperienced parents' point of view, it was disaster narrowly averted.

On this sultry, summer Sunday, the folks decided to go for a row down the river to the clam flats at Cockle Cove, a quarter mile away. It looked to be a dull morning. For a 10-year-old, rowing was about as exciting as watching grass grow. Rowing with my parents to go clamming, compounded the already dismal prospects. But there was no way out of it. Where my parents went, I went—like it or not. I usually liked it, but not this time. I twitched, I wiggled, I jiggled on that hard, narrow wooden front seat of the skiff. Every move brought a growl from my father.

"Sit still," he said.

"Don't move around so much."

"Level out the boat."

"SIT STILL!"

The greenheads with their stinging bites added another level of discomfort. As Wib rowed, the tall creekside marsh grasses swayed in the hot languid breezes, their tasseled and seed-heavy heads saluting the sun. Occasionally, a great blue heron laboriously lifted into the air, its raucous squawks interrupting the otherwise peaceful scene.

It was a very slow row that day. The monotonous *clunk-clunk, clunk-clunk* of the oars in the oarlocks was a metronome set on dead slow. The opposing tide made the interminable trip even slower. For every three feet we gained, the current took us back one foot. Eventually my father's patience, and he was a patient man, was rewarded. We reached the flats, and easily dug our 25 clams each. We then went for a swim and had our picnic lunch. All of this was fun, but overshadowing all was the deadly row home. The tide had turned, so that *oh so slow* ride had to be faced again. Apparently, my incessant fidgeting was too much for even my parents to bear.

"Dana, why don't you walk back to camp across the marsh," my dad said. *"We'll meet you back there. Go straight home now. No fooling around. No side trips."*

Hallelujah! Now they were talking. Going home across the marshes meant unlimited opportunities—opportunity to run, to explore, and to check out the whereabouts of the crow's nests. The young bird's characteristic gulping cries told me the nests were nearby. The marsh trip skirted the nesting area, and I could pinpoint their locations—handy knowledge for a 10-year-old.

The trip across the marsh started uneventfully. There's a particular art to running barefoot, unscathed and unpunctured through the needle-sharp marsh grasses. Any Cape Cod boy knows it. The occasional grass-free areas, though somewhat spongy in the middle, were fun to slide across, particularly with a running start. A larger than normal sliding area, about 15 feet across, suddenly came into view. I put on a burst of speed, slid across the first five or six feet then *sunk* to my waist in very soft mud. My head was now below the level of the surrounding grasses, out of sight to all save the birds.

I thought I was in quicksand and on my way to a watery death. No one would even know what had happened or where. I soon realized that I wasn't sinking, but my relief was tempered by the fact that I was in a very sticky situation. I was immobile and invisible, except to the cruising seagulls. There was no way to extricate myself. It would be hours before my folks would take alarm, and by then it would be dark. They were quite used to my frequent tardy arrivals.

To further compound my predicament, every horsefly in Chatham came to check out the newest offering in the marsh—a more or less stationary, pink cylinder of exposed flesh in the brown marsh mud. Mosquito bites itch. Horsefly bites hurt. A lot of horsefly bites hurt a lot. A mud overcoat was the only and obvious answer, so I lathered on the mud. I had an ample supply. The mud didn't do much for my appearance, but it relieved the frequency of those stinging bites.

Now I just had to get myself out of the mud, more struggles to no avail. As I quieted down and contemplated my situation, I became aware of some distant thunking noises on the landward side of the marsh. Through the tops of the swaying grasses, I could just make out a man chopping wood, a methodical *chunk, chunk, chunk* sound in the distance. Help was at hand, I thought. Maybe the woodsman could drag me out of this odoriferous ooze.

"Help! help! help!" I cried.

The man must have heard something. Maybe an errant eddy of wind carried my beseeching cry across the marsh. He stopped chopping, very deliberately put down the ax, stood on the chopping block, shaded his eyes and peered about the marsh. To his eyes, the marsh was empty. He gave it a long, thoughtful perusal. No matter how hard I yelled after that, there was no further response from him, save the *chunk, chunk, chunk* of the ax. I yelled, he chopped, and eventually he departed. My long distance companion was gone, and I was no closer to getting out. I was feeling desperate. The caked-on mud held the majority of the horseflies at bay, but how to get out of here?

Way off in the distance, coming through the grasses, a familiar sound seeped into my consciousness. Very faintly at first, then slowly louder, louder with each passing minute came the *clunk-clunk, clunk-clunk,* of those noisy oars. It had to be my folks rowing home, and not so far away. Now that oarlock sound was welcome. Oh, how welcome it sounded!

Whatever punishment I was going to receive, it had to be better than marinating in this fly-infested mudhole.

"HELP, HELP!"

It seemed strange to be yelling to my parents for help when I was ashamed to display my dilemma. The rowing stopped.

"HELP! Over here!"

"Betty, did you hear that?" my dad said. *"Sounds like Dana. Dana, is that you?"*

I could hear them anchoring the boat, and then their hurrying footsteps across the marsh. Their faces loomed above the grasses. When we parted I was five feet tall, a normal pink color, and all of a piece. What they now saw was only the top half of me, all layered with mud, hair in spikes and only my eyes and teeth showing normal coloration. There were muttered curses and imprecations of doom. Then the extraction began using oars, anchor ropes, and a seat from the skiff. There was much pulling, a lot of sucking noises, more mutterings (*"Maybe we should leave him here."*), and finally a very muddy 10-year-old was once more standing on the marsh bank and was promptly placed downwind. I was obviously happy to be out of the mud, my folks horrified by what might have happened.

Relief, Relief, Relief! Freedom to move again—a great feeling.

I dove into the river to shed my protective second skin, and a semblance of normalcy returned. But my parents still didn't want me in the boat. Once again the admonitions as to what would befall me if I strayed from a straight line walk back to the camp. My parents continued their row, while I set out again on foot, somewhat chastened, but not totally cowed. I arrived back at the camp in good order, but not without noting the exact whereabouts of those crow's nests.

The folks arrived and the discussion ensued. This was the same sort of discussion a drill sergeant would have with a bumbling recruit. The discussion concluded with: *"We have to go uptown to get some ice. We'll be back in a half hour or so. See if you can stay put til we get back. That means don't go anywhere. Don't move!"*

There wasn't much doubt about what they meant.

Raising Crow Chicks

But I kept thinking about those chicks. Once heard, the loud, gulping cry of a crow chick being fed is easily recognized. It sounds like nothing else. To this 10-year-old that cry was the siren song. In my mind, the edict, *"Don't move"* became don't move *much*, and *much* is a word with a lot of elasticity. Perhaps the nesting area was within the parameters of my instructions after all. And so off I went. High in the old pitch pines, I found six or eight nests, attended by a bevy of worried crow parents. The idea of raising a crow had much appeal. The thought of being followed by a flying companion was intriguing.

From my perspective, the *"don't move"* edict was already stretched pretty thin. Climbing up the tree to pick up a baby crow or two wouldn't stretch it much further. So up I went.

A startling aspect of life is how low heights look from the ground, and how high these same heights seem from the top. Those high nests seemed positively stratospheric when I was up there. That, coupled with the fact that the nests were very near the spindly tops of the trees, made for some shaky footing and many anxious moments. I reached over the edge of the nest, picked two of the largest half-grown chicks, and started down the tree to the accompaniment of the darting, screaming and furious adult crows.

The ascent had been tricky enough. The trip down the tree with two raucous, defecating half-grown crows was much more difficult. For the first half of the descent, I somehow managed. On the second half, gravity triumphed and down I came. A straight line is always the shortest distance between two points. My straight line flight path was interspersed with numerous branches and limbs, some of which I pruned and some of which did their best to prune me. But the baby crows had survived their first flight in fine shape. The flight instructor, on the other hand, suffered mightily—bruises, bumps, some ripped skin and torn muscle over my ribs, but nothing broken and nothing seriously hurt.

Once back at the camp, the chicks safely ensconced in a box, I couldn't wait to show my folks my newest treasures. It never occurred to me that the very existence of the birds in the box was obvious evidence of my stretching the *"don't move"* edict a bit. That oversight was corrected with the parents' return.

"Maybe we should have left him in the marsh," my dad said.

"Who is going to feed these things?" my mom replied.

Mothers tend to get to the core of things quickly. Consequently, I expected the worst. But it didn't come, save for the grounding edict. My parents, I think, took note of the puffy lump over my right eye, the blood oozing through my sweat shirt, and the black and blue decorations on my leg, and decided that I had been punished enough.

At any rate, being grounded for two weeks would give me time to learn how and what to feed the half-grown crows, and maybe teach them a few tricks. The fact that the crows would teach me never occurred.

The birds never really became pets. They did survive a diet of bread soaked in egg, and they eventually learned to fly after I ran them around the fields, raising and lowering them on my arm. They stayed around the camp for awhile, but their stays got shorter and shorter, the absences longer and longer, until they appeared no more. I remember being sad, but mostly relieved. The crows were back where they belonged, and I didn't have to care for them anymore.

A Man Of Few Words

While persistent, Cape Codders have a reputation for being

uncommunicative, and for some it was an earned reputation. "Yups" and "nopes" were considered conversation, and then only when silence wouldn't do. For example, as a young teen-ager, I worked 20 hours a week for a man that considered more than three words strung together the height of verbal extravagance. Chicky Clark was rarely extravagant. In a town of parsimonious talkers, Chicky was the most parsimonious.

My father wasn't exactly loquacious either.

I remember staying after school one day for some indiscretion or another. This was of no particular consequence except for the miles that separated the school and my house. Late buses were far in the future, so it was out on Route 28 with a soulful expression and my thumb in the air. It wasn't long before the guise of pitiful and maligned scholar did its trick. A funny little wreck of a car pulled up, and I hopped in for the ride to South Chatham five miles up the road. The driver said nothing, and so I looked out my side window, and said nothing, too. This was not unusual. Most men I knew said little, especially to kids. We rode along in companionable silence until I saw Pleasant Street. I pointed to the street.

"I live down there. Thanks for the lift," I said.

"I know," said a voice I recognized.

The driver was my father. He had borrowed a car for the day, and I hadn't recognized him.◆

The Essence Of Town

My paper route helped me to see the essence of our town. Delivering the old *Cape Cod Standard Times* took me, at age 13, to nearly all of the homes in South Chatham, east to west, north to south—from the spooky Zibrats on the west (spooky only because their house abutted a cemetery), to the home of good-hearted but taciturn Chicky Clark on the east.

One of my customers, Stella Eldredge, was an older, somewhat sharp-tongued lady whose father had "discovered" bay scallops, one of the most delicious shellfish in these waters. It is hard to believe that anything so delicious was ignored for so long. Scallops were abundant, easy to catch and yielded well. Before Mr. Eldredge's discovery, scallops had no value. They were in the same league that tomatoes had once been—inedible. In an attempt to find some use for the shellfish he had been tripping over and stepping on, Stella's father had tried all manner of experiments. To eat them whole, like shellfish, took the digestive tract of a seagull and inoperative taste buds. But old Mr. Eldredge figured there had to be some use for this plentiful creature. Since they grew in Chatham waters, they *had* to be useful. He was right. Finally, when he tried the abductor muscle alone, cooked or raw, he had the makings of a seasonal industry. Very few scallops have died of old age since.

There is very little that comes from the sea that equals a scallop's delightful and delicious taste. What a lot of pleasure this unsung hero's discovery has given us.

Another paper route customer, the Petersons, taught me a lasting lesson about how perception disguises reality. Their house was at the bottom of a steep hill on Route 28. Since two other customers lived behind them on the crest of a steep hill, it was easier and quicker to leave my bike at the foot of the hill and deliver the papers to the hilltop on foot. The Petersons lived in a modest house in marginal repair, and kept very much to themselves. Their curtains were usually drawn. They paid promptly (not everyone could afford the 35 cents on time), but rarely opened the door more than a crack to pay me. I'm not sure I ever saw the whole of either one of them. They were, to a young teenager, on the mysterious side—not frightening, but certainly *different* from most of my customers who usually had a cheery word for the paper boy. Just how wrong I was about these people was revealed to me one cold, windy, rainy day. I parked my bike, as usual, in the Petersons' front yard, delivered their paper to an outstretched hand in the partly-opened door, then sprinted up the hill with the other two papers. When I returned the bike was no longer on its kickstand, but rather it was leaning against the house. I didn't think much of it at the time, but as I continued on with the deliveries, I kept noticing some of the papers were wetter than they should have been. Some were even muddy. Like the coming of dawn, I realized what had happened. When I left the bike in the Petersons' front yard, the kickstand slowly sunk in the rain-softened ground, eventually overturning the bike. The papers slithered out of the bag and were blown around the wet, muddy yard. These quiet, kind people—the Petersons—saw this mess, and in the rain and wind came out to retrieve the errant papers, refold them, re-pack them and put the bike up against the house.

To me, they were still mysterious, but now they were *nice* mysterious. That door never did open more than the customary crack.

One of my favorite—and somewhat feared subscribers—was an antique dealer of no mean repute. Antiques were not the big business they are today. Elisha ran the business out of his home. Most every afternoon, you could find him sitting in the big Morris chair over by the west window, waiting for his paper and the paper boy. Elisha was a born storyteller, and I was the sole audience. He had one on-going story of how as a youngster he used to swim to Monomoy six miles distant, dig a bushel of clams, swim the clams and himself back home, and do it all before school. The story expanded to include his carrying a stove to cook a batch of clams enroute, and because meals are best with a dessert, he let it be known that he figured out how to bake a cake to finish off the journey. Elisha was a man to reckon with and respect as well, at least in his story telling.

I'll never forget that Halloween night when my friend Warren and I were harassing him from the shelter of a nearby hedge. We had done this the year before, and our efforts had been met with a delightful barrage of obscenities unleashed at full volume in the quiet October air, as we scuttled away chortling. This year, though, our chortles turned to terror when Elisha appeared from behind us and grabbed Warren by the scruff of the neck:

"Now you little bastard, I've gotcha," he proclaimed. *"You'll be sorry you ever messed with my house, but you won't be sorry long. I'm going to cut your (expletive) head off!"*

With those chilling words, Warren was dragged face-down across the driveway, to the back of Elisha's house. There, artfully arranged in the pool of light by the back door, stood the chopping block! Embedded in the block was a big red ax with a shiny cutting edge. Warren squealed and wiggled for a little while, but to no avail. A vigorous shake or two reduced him to limpness. As they approached the chopping block, the imprecations increased about how high the blood would spurt and how far Warren's head would roll. Elisha made a great show of trying to get the ax out of the block with one hand and appeared not to be able to do it. He dropped Warren with a growled admonition. *"Don't move an inch,"* he warned. As soon as Warren's feet hit the ground, he and I hit the road at flank speed. Had anyone timed us, we probably would have set some kind of world record for long distance sprinters. From that night on, we respected old Elisha, but ever after warily and at a distance. Never again did we visit his house on Halloween.

But not all my customers were as imaginative as Elisha or as mysterious as the Petersons. Most of them were as kind as could be, putting up with my sometimes erratic deliveries, enticing me with cookies instead of curses, and generally making my life a pleasant journey.

A Mess Of Flounders

South Chatham is flanked by salt water on three sides. It has Eel Pond and Eel River bordering most of the eastern side, Nantucket Sound bathing the south side, and Red River guarding the western border. As geography goes that combination is hard to beat.

We spent a lot of our time in the pleasurable pursuit of things piscatorial, which is a long-winded way of saying we went fishing a lot. Fishing pays dividends all out of proportion to the effort expended. Fishing gives one an excuse to own a boat. While you don't need a boat, having one makes the chances of catching a few fish much more likely. Another dividend is the deep satisfaction of bringing home a meal (or two or more) from the bounty of the sea. Then best of all is the taste of very fresh fish—bluefish fillets or bass cooked over the coals the day it was caught. It's good stuff—ambrosia. But few fish taste as good as the spring run of flounder. This low-slung, low-lying, plebeian fish is one of my favorites. Its taste is to finfish as scallops are to shellfish, the best.

The pursuit of flounders demonstrated a salty side of my father's character. One beautiful April day Wib decided it was about time to get a mess of flounders. Did mother and I want to come along? Well, of course we did. So we went to Eel Pond in South Chatham, a known hot spot for flounders in the spring, launched the skiff, an old wooden basket (a local term for leaker), and rowed out to the drop-off where we knew the flounders lurked. Flounders are fished just off the bottom with a bit of quahog as bait. A drop line is the only tackle, a simple and inexpensive rig—our kind of rig. It wasn't long before the characteristically tentative tugs of soft-mouthed flounders began. Some fish bite with a no-nonsense yank, others with very soft, almost uncertain nibbles. Flounders are in this latter category. It takes a small amount of experience to know when to strike a flounder—too soon and you pull the bait right out of their mouths, wait too long and they have taken the bait and departed, probably with a little flounder chuckle.

We anchored that day where we could see our parked car sitting all by itself in the dirt parking lot at the end of a remote dirt road. It was where we always parked it when we fished the Eel Pond or its environs. We were quite happy; we were catching fish and anticipating a succulent fillet or two for dinner. At the rate the flounders were coming over the rail, we would have enough to give my grandparents a few. We always gave whole flounders away; the recipient was expected to do his own filleting.

So there we were, catching spring's bounty, basking in the sunshine when a distant sound galvanized my father in a way I'd never seen before. The sound was the muted rumble of *our* car starting.

Before our incredulous eyes, someone turned our car around and drove up the road into the woods and out of sight. My normally phlegmatic parents unphleged fast:

"(Expletive) Betty, did you see that? What in hell is going on? Where did that guy come from?"

This was quite a revelation to me. I didn't know my Dad could swear. We rowed back to the landing at full speed, unloaded the fishing gear, and my parents tried to *will* the car back to its rightful place. There was a lot of talk between them about the wisdom of tossing the keys in the glove compartment as a deterrent to theft, the usual post mortem talk of any unpleasant, preventable action.

The biggest mystery was *who* took the car and *where* did they come from. A major clue was a small cabin cruiser tied to a nearby dock. It was not there when our fishing expedition started. As we were milling around in puzzlement, father let loose another blast of what to me was a new and delightful aspect of his character:

"(Expletive) Betty, I hear the car coming back. What in merry hell is going on?"

And sure enough over the hill and down the old road came the errant car going faster than my father ever drove it. The driver pulled up in a flurry of dust, hopped out and in the faces of my two outraged parents, blithely said:

"Hey, you leave your keys in the same place I do. I just had to go uptown to get a new fanbelt for the boat. When I get her fixed how would you folks like to go for a test ride?"

This was it. I knew this guy was in for a reaming, for fury unleashed. Nobody ever borrowed anything without permission, ever. The explosion never came. The stranger's guileless explanation overcame what I expected to be the blowup of the century—overcame it to the extent that ten minutes after the return of the car, the man was treating us to a ride in the newly fan-belted boat, and father had resorted to his usual phlegmatic self.

I had discovered a salty side of Wib's character and also discovered there were aspects of adult behavior that I (at the age of ten) didn't begin to comprehend. How did that guy get away with taking the family car and not paying dearly for it, without even an admonition? It was remarkable to me—those mysterious rites of adults.

An Invasion

The turbulent 40s brought the doings of the outside world much closer to our cloistered Cape. First my oldest uncle was called away for service in Europe. Then the youngest uncle was called up; soon his letters were talking about the Philippine Islands. And my dad was in the Coast Guard Reserve; he and his crew patrolled Nantucket Sound in small boats on a weekly basis.

The chaff of war began washing up on our beaches. Gobs of tar-like crude oil from torpedoed ships and bits and pieces of airplane aluminum came in with the tides. Ships were sunk just off our shores — their entrails littered Monomoy's east shore. Those leaving spoke eloquently of the war engulfing our nations and our world.

But war's leftovers do not speak as eloquently as war's reality. What brought this global conflict's immensity to my world occurred in the mid-40s. On a bright and clear morning, about dawn, we heard a sound unlike any we had heard before. A deep house-shaking rumbling woke us. Six tanks went up our little used road, going at a goodly speed — no sign of soldiers, just six purposeful, buttoned-up tanks roaring up Pleasant Street. For this 12-year-old, it was heady stuff. I gulped breakfast, called Warren, and we set off for the beach, a half mile distance. Warren too had seen the tanks. He strapped on his hunting knife, and I loaded my Red Ryder BB-gun. We wanted to be ready to repel any attackers.

The tanks with their rumble were gone, but the closer we got to the beach another much more pervading rumble dominated our senses. As we crested the last hill before the beach, we saw more boats, more ships, than Nantucket Sound has ever seen — before or since. There were big gray ships a mile or two out, and mottled amphibious craft were scuttling back and forth to shore. And wondrous to behold, there were at least hundreds, more likely, thousands of men in combat gear on the beaches. They were in foxholes with rifles and machine guns. They were in mortar emplacements. There were ambulances. There were all manner of trucks and jeeps roaring around — all the trappings of war right on our unsullied beaches. The South Chatham-South Harwich town line was well and truly invaded.

It was a war game, practice for the real thing. We apparently were the only resistance — one armed with a hunting knife, the other with a Red Ryder BB-gun. They easily won us over. The first solder we met wanted to borrow the BB-gun. I had been taught to never, under any circumstance, aim any gun — BB or otherwise — at anyone. I was awestruck when he proceeded to plink away at a sleeping buddy ten feet away. I can still hear the pellets bouncing off that steel helmet. More impressive yet was the language of the awakened soldier. He used words I had never heard before, words that unmistakably expressed displeasure at all around him. The troops had a rough tolerance for us. They showed us all their equipment, shared their C rations with us, and I'm sure, envied our innocence and our youth.

To the soldiers, this practice was probably boring. Army maneuvers are usually that. Certainly, we kids didn't have much conceptions of the reality behind the "invasion" of South Chatham, or any inkling that just a decade later, we also would be struggling with our feelings, with some of the very same equipment on the other side of the globe. There, too, as we practiced our maneuvers, that nation's youngsters were the onlookers. But for us 12-year-old kids, the war games at the end of Pleasant Street were just high entertainment, played for our enjoyment. In our minds, we knew the world would always stay the same, just as we knew beaches were always playgrounds.

'Snow Was A Given'

Nature provided us with entertainment year-round. In the winter, unique avenues of play opened up with the onslaught of cold weather. Winters were colder in those days, "skateable" ice on the ponds and bogs was a given for at least four-to-six weeks. Snow was a given. Come November, we were ready for the first of it, and nature rarely disappointed.

With the fall of snow, most of South Chatham had acres and acres of an unblemished white coverlet — a coverlet that soon became decorated with the thin parallel lines of sled runners and punctuated with the footsteps of children. Every hill within walking distance soon had a beaten down run on its flanks.

Winter brought greater solitude to an already quiet side of town. South Chatham became positively mute. The silence of the snow covered land was all but absolute. The land was a stage set for children's enjoyment.

One such stage was the flooded bogs. Cranberry bogs are often flooded late in the fall to prevent weed seeds from taking root. This also provided a fairly shallow skating surface. We called it "skating." It was actually an approximation of skating, an icy sport with wobbly skates, runny noses, constant bumps and unremitting falls. Often with a rock and a stick from the woods, we played a game that none of us had seen, only heard about—something called hockey.

But what stands out most in my mind is the memory of 10 or 15 people zooming around on the ice, the shrieks of the girls and the laughter of all the sideliners cheering on the horseplay. This play was an age eraser at a time of life when a few years made a big difference in the available friends. Skating brought out everyone, young and old. Whoever was available came down to that frozen bog for the fun, and occasionally to dare the "main ditch."

A cranberry bog is bisected by a grid of ditches. The smaller secondary ditches drain into the main canal. Falling through the ice over a secondary ditch was a damp but trifling thing. At the very worst, you might get soaked up to your waist—by no means life threatening, only uncomfortable. Almost always, a fire was going in the adjacent sandpit to take care of such soggy extremities.

Falling through the main ditch was a much different matter. This ditch was deep, often well over our heads, and usually had running water which thinned the ice unpredictably. This moving water had the added hazard of being able to carry you under the adjacent ice if you happened to fall in. Often where the main ditch spilled over the dike and where it was the deepest, there was no ice at all, just black ominous water. It was water that looked quietly at you and said:

"In here kid, you die."

But what kid could resist an attraction like that, especially with the neighborhood girls looking on. One after another we'd dare the "main ditch." Each mark of the previous skater was a taunt to the next, to go closer, a little closer to that quiet, ominous, black, rippling water. None of us ever fell in. The tone and frequency of the cracking ice was a warning that we dared, but also heeded.

Our skating had little grace, no style. It was all energy, eagerness and enthusiasm—wobbly ankles, dull skates (it was quite a few years before I even knew skates could be sharpened) and determination, all accompanied by numerous collisions with that glittering, unyielding ice. It is hard to fall any quicker than while skating. One second you are up, and at least in your mind's eye, gracefully swirling around the ice, the next—by some strange alchemy—you are flat on the ice with no idea how this sorry state of affairs came about. It's most puzzling. The pain and bruises come later, and they aren't puzzling at all. They just hurt.

If the fall wasn't too obvious, it was considered cool to lie on your stomach and study the goings on under the ice. Perhaps even call over another skater to show him the marvels taking place under the glass clear ice. Then maybe the onlookers might think your supine position was not a result of your making a fool of yourself but lo, you were sprawled on the ice studying nature. Of course, if you had bloodied your nose by smacking it on that rock hard surface, it was much more difficult to carry off the guise of the pseudo-scientist. Then it was best to just lie there and hope no one noticed you discoloring the ice.

An aspect of skating that lingers in the mind is the sight of that roaring fire that seemed to encompass such an aura of delight and was so much a part of the nighttime skating parties. Those whose ankles wouldn't support them any longer kept that blaze well lit. The big logs for sitting made a dark border around the yellow-red fire. The column of bright yellow sparks appeared as swirling bits of leftover sunlight, disappearing high in the black sky. The moving patterns of color, as the brightly clad skaters whirled in and out of that circle of light, was as a life-sized kaleidoscope—a Currier & Ives brought to life. An added fillip, if the fire had been built on the ice, was the slowly expanding pool of water around the base of the fire. This pool was full of gray ashes, black chunks of partially burned wood, steaming firebrands, and an occasional wet bottom as some skater, more awkward than most, slid through the mess on his fanny, to the delighted teasing of all.

Another sport that winter brought was sledding. The Cape's snows blanketed the skating parties and opened the door to sledding. Outdoors every negative was balanced with a positive. We used to go over to South Harwich to a place we called the "hospital" and to another area close by called the "meadow." But the best hill around was down by the Eel Pond about a half mile away. This run was in under trees, so it took a healthy snowstorm to provide good sliding. Two or three times a winter, nature would oblige and the good times would happen, and occasionally, this was a multi-generational happening, particularly on Sunday. The rules of deferential behavior towards adults was suspended, everyone was just having a good time. The run swerved down between the pitch pines, emerged into a small opening, then flattened out by the pond edge in a patch of scraggly bushes. The first order of business was to pack down the snow, a fun project that involved walking up and down the run a few times then taking progressively longer trials with the sled to beat down the errant snow. In short order the "run" was established and the sliding began in earnest.

It was usually contests: whose sled could go the farthest, the fastest and who could get closest to that big tree near the end of hill.

We took turns singly at first, then two to a sled barreling down the hazard strewn track. The faster you went, the more ominous the trees. We met most of the trees flanking the trail, met them resoundingly to the accompaniment of groans and moans. Nothing polite about these meetings—just a thud, a flurry of snow, a groan or two, then it was back up the hill to plan another faster downhill assault. We occasionally tried three to a sled, three bodies stacked up like three logs, but we rarely made it to the bottom. With three, the lag time was too great. By the time the top body was leaning left, the other two were going right. The only good thing about a three-stack was there was always plenty of company when the inevitable pileup occurred.

When the adults could and would join in it was a magical time. The shrill laughter of the children was leavened with the deeper laughter of the adults. Sledding somehow erased the gulf between adults and children. It seemed in every phase of life the older people always knew better than any of us kids. Except sledding. The sight of one of these adults rolling around in the snow after bouncing off a tree, coming up snow covered and grinning was an equalizer of some magnitude. I looked forward to seeing the "big ones" ricochet off one of the numerous hazards, and come up snow covered and laughing—a generational eraser of the first order.

Something that we could use today.

Lots of spills meant snow driven up pant legs, down necks and up sleeves all of which eventually dulled the desire for more of the same. Then the walk that seemed so short on the way over, stretched interminably ahead. How good the heat of home seemed. The cold always put up a good fight to stay, really dug in its heels, but never did the pain of thawing lessen our desire to get out the old Flexible Flyer when next it snowed. Thawing was an ordeal. Winter involved a lot of thawing, both of the bodies and of the generational differences. The one was painful, the other pure pleasure.◆

On The Water

⌒∽

Chatham High School was located just upstairs from the elementary grades. The first six grades were located on the first floor of the building; grades seven through twelve were on the second floor. The cafeteria and woodworking shops were located in the basement. In my graduating class, 23 of us high-spirited clam diggers walked across the stage to the world beyond Chatham.

But not before thoroughly sampling all that Chatham had to offer. For most of us, Chatham was defined by our immediate neighborhood—at least prior to our getting a car. The acquisition of a driver's license and an old fliver changed all that. Christmas Day, shortly after I turned sixteen, was momentous. One of my presents was a five dollar bill (the cost of a driver's license) and a note from Grampa Eldridge promising instruction in driving. This was long before Driver's Education came along. Although I didn't appreciate it, my horizons were about to expand beyond my imagination. My balloon tired, well-used bicycle was about to gather dust.

A driver's license and an old '33 Dodge coupe melted the moat of miles. On my own, I could now easily reach Stage Harbor and Monomoy across the harbor. Pleasant Bay was now just a short drive away, and new friends were around the corner. My "neighborhood" expanded from South Chatham to Chatham, then to all the Cape, and with a little imagination, it would include all of North America. At first, just exploring the many dirt roads was adventure enough.

Freedoms unheard of today were taken for granted then. There weren't enough of us to despoil the landscape to any great degree. The environment was not a consideration, and so we "explored" it to the fullest, to the brink of no return.

"How are we going to get out of here?" "This is the end, Eldridge. We're never going to move this heap."

I knew things looked a little bleak, but "heap?" This was a fine car. It looked as though it was submerging. Of course, it wasn't, but it did look like it was about to become a permanent decoration on the northern edge of Goose Pond.

Late one evening after a hard day's work, the two Keene boys and I decided to head for this accommodating pond for a clean-up wash and swim. When we arrived, we noticed the water level was quite low. It had been a very dry summer and more beach was showing than we'd ever seen. As kids are wont to do, a dare was proffered:

"I bet you can't drive all the way around the pond."

"Sure looks low enough."

"Bet we can."

Nobody asked why we were doing it. In a teenager's world, *why* we did things was something we only thought of *if* what we were doing didn't work. Asking *why* before the event was the parents' mode, not ours.

The challenge of driving all the way around the pond was exciting, and as far as we knew no one had ever done it. That alone made it worth doing in our minds. The fact that it was dark also helped. Our few inhibitions were well muted. We pulled left on the narrow beach, and let her go. Not bad, not bad at all. The damp sand was firm, the old car motored right along. As we became bolder, we picked up speed and were having a high old time. Going around this pond would be a breeze, we thought. Why hadn't we thought of this before? The car roared and bounced. We laughed and yelled.

But the beach was narrowing, narrowing to the point that our right wheels were beginning to splash water now and again. Soon the wheels were always in the water. We finally woke up to the fact that the pond edge was right at the sandy cliff face, and that we would not make it around the pond that night. Our enthusiasm had carried us well beyond prudence.

By now all four wheels were in the water, and because of the slope of the pond bottom, the car was stuck much deeper on the right. We tried turning around by backing into the cliff face. We made it half way before the car's engine started to race, and the car stopped. At this point the water was over the front bumper.

Manual shift cars have clutches, and clutches work on friction.

With enough friction, the car will move. We soon figured out what had happened. The car was in deep enough to let water get on the clutch plate. With no friction, there was no movement. To add to our increasingly difficult predicament, the engine was starting to miss a beat now and then. When we lifted the hood, it was all blue sparks and spray. The car had settled enough for the fan belt to pick up water and anoint the engine liberally. The wires were shorting out. We couldn't move, the engine was dying, we were five miles from home, and I needed the car first thing next morning to go to work—to say nothing of the fact that the we were directly in front of someone's cottage. It was at this point that the imprecations were coming thick and fast.

"We'll never get this thing out of here."

"You're an idiot, Eldridge."

"Whose idea was this anyway?"

While we were pondering our position, one, two and then a third turtle surfaced in the headlight's flickering glimmer. Those three turtles, for all a turtle's reputation for slowness, were a lot more mobile than we were. A good laugh at ourselves helped break the log jam of gloomy thoughts. We jammed some debris against the accelerator to get the engine racing; let some air out of the tires until they felt spongy (I can still hear the air bubbling up through the water); put the gearshift in reverse; and the three of us got ready to push whenever the clutch decided to dry itself out.

It took a while. The turtles cruised about in the headlight's feeble glow, the engine hiccuped and burped, sparks flew, water flew, and we waited. Eventually with a shudder, a jolt, another jolt, the clutch caught, we pushed, and the car slammed back into the cliff face and stalled. But stalled wasn't bad. The car was now in a position to be driven out. Saved again. We said good-bye to the turtles (who by making us laugh got us thinking again), and drove back along the pond edge. We had a subdued swim and cleanup, and headed home.

I know turtles are long lived, but I don't know if turtles have a sense of humor or not. If they do, check out the Goose Pond some August at about 10:30 pm, one half mile east of the landing by that steep cliff face. Listen carefully (turtle laughter is very quiet) for an old gray bearded turtle telling the younger turtles about the kids who tried to take a car for a swim: how funny they looked when the car shot out from under them and slammed into the sand bank; how the three boys fell on their faces in the knee deep water and exited laughing.

"Fearsome Beating"

Every winter the Cape's east shore, the "backside" of old, takes a fearsome pounding. Each year the abrasive effect of those raging easterlies consumes several feet off our coast from Monomoy Point to Provincetown. These violent storms leave a "new snow" type of beach. No footprints mar the wave-washed shore. Later, walkers find the battered lobster pots that escaped last fall's haul-out. Their sojourn in the raging sea takes its toll. The traditional wooden pots that wash up on the spring shore are gap-toothed skeletons of their original construction, and the wire pots that wash up are badly bent caricatures of their former function. They are reminders that the ocean's might is not to be trifled with, that the winter ocean is a beast far different from the summer ocean with its gentle ways and soothing sounds. Try to tame a winter ocean, any ocean, and your attempts will be cast ashore out of hand—much as many lobster pots, mistakenly left to winter, end up as debris on the outer beaches.

The beach profile changes over the course of a year. The early spring beach is a flat beach. The summer profile is a wide high beach with a fairly steep drop-off from the high tide to the low tide line—the sculptor, the benign breezes of summer. Winter and early spring beaches are crafted by a more violent hand. The profile of the winter beach is flat. The dune base is the high tide line, with the low tide line often 300 or 400 feet away across a flotsam-free, sterile looking, strip of sand. Winter beaches come by their profile naturally—that savaging northeast wind hits Cape Cod after jousting with the folks in Nova Scotia. This wind then slides unfettered down across the Gulf of Maine, gathering speed and energy on the way. Then, as if affronted by the land mass in its path, the wind slams into the bended arm of Cape Cod, as two giants arm wrestling. Every joust leaves the Cape extant but the price is high. Like Shylock's Portia and the "pound of flesh," the Cape too, is in a poor bargaining position. The price for surviving those eroding easterlies is about five acres of its soul (soil) a year, and to paraphrase Will Rogers, nowhere on Cape Cod are they making more land.

In geologic terms, the Cape is very young. Scientists now think this peninsula has been delighting man or beast for only about 20,000 years. In less than 5,000 years, it will all be gone. Twenty five thousand years is just the merest blip in geologic time.

Cape Cod is easy prey for the ocean. It juts out to sea and takes whatever the elements deal out. Next to water, sand is the easiest thing to move, and the Cape is nothing if not sand. Rocks are so scarce here that we name them, as if by naming them they—and maybe we—will achieve some permanence.

I don't think in geologic terms very often. It is much more comforting to think in human terms where a 100-year-old life span is something to talk about. In a long lifetime, the Cape will lose about 500 acres. This is a human-sized fact, and one easier to deal with than the eventual demise of the entire Cape thousands of years hence. The bright side of this relentless erosion is that eventually every house, however mean, will be "waterfront!" If it's your house today, enjoy the view but remember the *Merchant of Venice* analogy, and get the "For Sale" sign ready.

The ocean is one of nature's artisans, constantly wearing away whatever is in its path, making rough contours smooth, submerging all before it. One positive effect of this relentless erosion is change. Never do we see the same Cape Cod. Every convulsion of nature rearranges our "face" to the sea. Every day, the sea no matter how calm, moves and shuffles the sand grains, taking a little here, a little there. The net result is more change.

I have a son in the Rocky Mountains. He has a magnificent view of those craggy peaks, but if he lives to be 100-years-old, those peaks will wear down only a hair's width. Here, if you live to be 100, rivers have been shut off, beaches have been moved or broken through, clam beds have come and gone. Change is the only constant on Cape Cod.

One thing that hasn't changed much in my lifetime is the fearsome and often vertical waters at the south end of Monomoy. Some of the sand sloughed off the east side of Cape Cod eventually finds its way south and forms a rip off the end of Monomoy Island.

Point Rip is a name that conjures up a multitude of memories — a place where the sandy finger of Monomoy stretches closest to

Nantucket's Great Point, a place where some of the most dangerous waters of the Atlantic coast are in constant turmoil, a place that harbors the fighting bluefish and is home to the turbulence-loving striped bass. For six hours or so of the rising tide, the cold, clear waters of the Atlantic sweep westward around the end of Monomoy into Nantucket Sound, and for the following six hours or so, the plankton-rich waters of Nantucket Sound push eastward into the cold Atlantic. This back and forth motion creates and maintains an underwater ridge of sand that hooks a considerable distance towards Nantucket. On any given day, at any given time, the ocean may be calm, Nantucket Sound may be calm, but almost always, the Rip lives up to its name.

From shore or the sea, the meeting of these two very dissimilar bodies of water produces the dramatic spectacle of two mindless titanic entities slugging it out. For six hours that cold, implacable ocean is triumphant, surging its might into the sound. Then back comes the resilient Bay pushing the intrusive ocean back east where it belongs with a row of breaking waves marking the line of battle.

This underwater ridge of sand, this back and forth surge of waters, produces an "edge," a prime spot for the game fish of summer to congregate and to feed on the baitfish. And congregate they do. Monomoy's Point Rip is probably the most likely place to look for blues or bass on any summer or fall day.

The shorebound watcher, sitting on a beach grass covered dune on a typical summer day with a gentle southwest wind blowing in his face, would be seeing the inspiration of impressionists—with the bright green of the summer grasses, the bright white of the ocean-rimming sand, and the shadings of green, greenish-blue, to deep blue of the ocean's increasing depths. And dominating all, the ever-changing, boisterous, rioting Point Rip with its line of snowy white breaking waves. It can be a spellbinding scene. No real surprises, you pretty much know what is going to happen, but a riveting sight nonetheless. It is a sight, if one had to pay for beauty, that we couldn't afford.

The Rip from a boat is another matter entirely. No matter how you arrive, the shortest distance the boat could have traveled is 10 miles, and if it is summer, almost certainly 10 calm miles. The Rip itself is rarely more than 200 feet wide, but those 200 feet will be much rougher than the preceding ten miles. It's not the height of the waves that grabs your attention, as much their proximity to each other. These are very friendly waves, wanting to join you in your boat. They also have a tendency to lose their heads. It's those six or eight foot waves, side by side, cheek by jowl, with their roaring, crashing, breaking crests that can so easily lap aboard and jar you out of the routine of that 10-mile uneventful boat ride. This Rip has been known to stir boat drivers from near somnolence to near terror in a boat's length.

We don't seem to respect much these days, but nobody has lost any respect for that ferocious strip of violent water. It doesn't change, it's rough all the time. It's ready to terrify the unwary and sink the unwise.

Perhaps the fascination with these violent natural spectacles is the likeness to life itself — long periods of calm, punctuated by short periods of turbulence and bits of terror, and the resolve to be more careful in the future. It is the fear, relief and the knowledge that you have adequately handled a boat in these wild waters, that you have survived. There is beauty, too — the calm blue-green waters juxtaposed with the breaking, hissing, foaming waves showing bright white in sunlight. There is a joy of being alive to see such sights, to experience such sounds. The Rip has it all, and therein lies its attraction and magnificence.

Not all boats survive that turbulence. One of my first intimations that life doesn't always have a happy ending came when my folks returned from a Monomoy duck hunting trip with grim news.

Two close family friends in their early 20s — Tom and "Let" — had decided that the lure of the thousands of sea ducks feeding on the mussel beds off the east side of Monomoy was too strong to resist. They had been out there the day before and had done well. The next afternoon they launched their small, flat-bottomed, wooden skiff in all but calm seas halfway down Monomoy's east side. They invited my father along, but he thought the boat looked a little small for three, and he opted to wait until the next trip. Tom and Let rowed out to bag some easy game just off the tranquil beach. The waters were calm, but the current was swift, and the anchor line inadequate. They were powerless against Monomoy's four knot current, and were swept south towards turbulent Point

Rip, a mile or so away. They were carried close past the Stone Horse Lightship yelling for help. There was nothing the lightship men could do but watch and shout encouragement. Lightships are stationary; they are designed to stay in one place no matter what. My folks, watching from shore, saw the desperate trouble their friends were in. They tried to drive the old beach car to the Monomoy Point station to get help. When it became hopelessly stuck, they ran, in boots, in the soft beach sand a mile and a half to the station, and gasped out their story.

The Coast Guard readied the rowing surfboat, while my folks were escorted to the lookout at the top of the station; on that day, it was a wonderful vantage point with a terrible view. The Point Rip was in full uproar—those steep, tightly-ranked waves that seem to defy gravity were in serried rows like dragon's teeth. With powerful binoculars my folks saw the tiny skiff and their two good friends being relentlessly carried into this devil's cauldron—over one impossible wave, over another, then nothing. The searching Coast Guard boat found nothing. Days later, the overturned skiff was found floating placidly not far from the Rip. Now, every year those heavy-bodied sea ducks return, and in my mind, bring Tom and Let—forever 25—back with them. I never go through the Rip without thinking this is the last thing these two young men ever saw. And as I get older, I give a little salute to them on each passage. While I didn't know Let that well, Tom was a friend—irrepressible and fun. He used to bring me bird cards. These were the small colored cards with a picture of a bird on one side and some life history on the other. These little cards kindled my desire for a career in the natural sciences. Thank you, Tom.

Complete Solitude

Very few experiences on the water lead to an early death. The vast majority of these waterborne excursions are pleasurable. Sunrises, sunsets, most any view is amplified and enhanced by sitting in a boat. There is something about the chuckling of water, the gentle rocking motion, and the clean smell of salt water that somehow makes the view better. I only know if offered the choice of a seat on shore or on a boat, I'd go for the boat every time. Come experience a typical summer evening's drift in tranquil Pleasant Bay.

Cape Cod has nooks and crannies aplenty. The summer throngs come and seemingly stretch the Cape's capacity to absorb people. But those numerous nooks have always enabled us to eat the evening meal in complete solitude, drifting languidly across Little Pleasant Bay at the behest of the breeze. If the bluefish insist and break water right beside the boat, we will sometimes bestir ourselves and take one home for the next evening's meal, or, in the interest of tranquillity, just watch their antics. Out there on the bay, we have seen many spectacular sunsets, seen schools of small bass chasing bait in water so shallow their backs were out of water, and watched baby foxes gambol on a hillside while their weary mother lay stretched supine on a convenient log. But with no sunset, with no aquatic display, and with no bonus of playful foxes, the solitude itself is delightful, particularly after the hustle and bustle of a summertime Cape Cod. In the light wind, the boat will swing broadside and the small waves will produce a gentle lapping along the waterline. It's a most welcome counterpoint to summer's commotion.

On a typical warm summer evening's drift, we sit in the boat and look around the horizon, the panorama around the compass. Almost due south is the recurring flash of Chatham Light. We wonder who else is being stroked by its beams—fishermen off Chatham surely, or recreational boaters perhaps anxiously looking for something discernible on their charts. That two million candlepower light is discernible all right, as is its flashing sequence. Pilots of small planes certainly see the light from the air. The revolving beams resemble nothing so much as turning spokes, no rim on that wheel of light. The light sweeps us on the gently bobbing boat, but its sweeping moves not a particle of matter.

A bit farther to the west is a bright arc of light. The Chatham baseball or soccer team is bathed in the powerful outdoor lights that resemble, from this distance, a remnant of leftover daylight that got lost and didn't follow the sunset. If you follow the source of those lights back far enough—to the fossil fuels of its inception— it really is leftover daylight.

Somewhere just west of this illuminated playing field is the grave of William Nickerson, founder of the town of Chatham. His gravesite sits high above the Bay. I like to think his spirit is looking across the Bay at me from time to time.

Scattered along the Bay shore are the twinkling lights of the numerous homes, all lived in, all enjoyed. The affect of these lights, viewed from a few miles away across the water is as though a few errant stars decided to settle on the shores of this lovely Bay. They sparkle and twinkle, and eventually flicker out as the evening progresses.

Over there in the southwest by South Chatham is a high flashing red light that shines from a 300-foot receiving antenna of the MCI complex—the same antenna that first received word of the Andrea Doria-Stockholm collision off Nantucket.

Further around the horizon, over in back of Strong Island, a large dull glow backlights the island and portions of the bay. Harwich must have a ballgame on tonight, too. It's hard to keep those Harwich Hairleggers down. Just a bit farther around the Bay and almost due west, a bright cheery cluster of lights identifies Wequassett Inn by Round Cove where my great uncle Carrol Nickerson, after a lifetime as a sailing commercial fisherman, came closest to drowning. He fell through the salt ice on an eeling expedition, and darn near didn't make it to shore

In the northwesterly quadrant, a bevy of red blinking lights makes the horizon look less benign, more official somehow. Orleans and Brewster water towers, radio transmitting towers and TV receiving towers project into the night sky, an affront to this peaceful skyline. Against these lights, dim shapes of the glacial moraine show their sinuous outlines. Moving clockwise, still another remnant of leftover daylight up towards the northwest horizon tells us that Orleans, too, is having a ball game.

Looking way around to the northeast we see a bobbing, weaving set of lights, first high in the sky, then briefly just a muted glow, then a sweeping arc across the warm night sky. It has to be a beach buggy bumping its way over the flotsam and jetsam on the beach. Just east of us on a nearby island, a bevy of fireflies stitch the night sky together with threads of light. I like the fireflies best. They produce the most light, most efficiently, for a more fundamental purpose. They make our efforts at illumination seem puny. All the fireflies are trying to do is attract a mate. They obviously succeed. They come back every year to hemstitch the night with light—a welcome sign of summer. Such is a typical summer's evening on Pleasant Bay.

Sooner or later, the cool of the evening replaces the heat of the day, and our reverie takes on a more practical slant. It is time to start the motor and turn the bow towards home. The motor intrudes on the quiet. The spell of the Bay is over for this time, though we are ready, willing and waiting to be bewitched again and again.◆

Down On Schooner Bar

Each season on the Cape has its own sounds. Summer sounds are soft, fall is heralded by the clarion call of high geese, winter moans with a bitter north wind, and spring echoes with a cacophony of noises. On windless nights each spring, we hear a popping noise down by the big rock on the edge of the pond. It marks the arrival of small striped bass that each year come to this rock where the tide eddies deliver bait fish to their hungry mouths. The noise they make in the consumption is remarkably like a small boy slurping spaghetti. Probably the bait fish taste as good to the bass as the spaghetti does to the boy. Whatever the reason, spring evenings on the pond are punctuated by the in-drawn popping noise of feeding bass—a sound delightful for its promise.

The small bass seem to venture far up the estuaries, some perhaps to the fresh water of their origins, for the food and safety these quieter waters provide. As these same fish get larger, they forgo this protection for greater feeding opportunities in wilder ocean waters where schools of sand eels congregate.

The striped bass goes by many names—striper, ole linesides, Roccus, and Morone. Whatever the name, it is a magnificent fish. Nature designed him to feed in the roil of the surf. His broad body and that powerful wide tail give him all the strength and agility he needs to loll in the backwash of the surf, to devour the baitfish that are tumbled in this cascading water. On Monomoy I've seen them many times in the toss of the breaking waves, their silver-green backs momentarily out of water. Out on the sand bars in minimal depths of water, these masters of turbulence, half awash, pursue the darting sand eels. It is a sight that excites the most lethargic fisherman.

Down on Schooner Bar at dusk one day, I saw just such a sight, huge bass rolling on the wave-tossed bar, half out of water, angling for one of its favorite foods, the sand eel. These big fish were oblivious to all else; their focus was food. They were about 50 yards out and I had the spot all to myself—fishing perfection in the low light of setting sun. The beauty of the scene was enjoyment enough, with the white sands of the deserted beach turning pink in the sunset, the blue ocean slowly turning black as the night stole the light, and as an accompaniment, acres of those 30-pound eel eaters right at my feet. It seemed like the opportunity of a lifetime. At $5 each ($25 today), I could in a few hours pick up some much needed cash for the college year ahead. All I had to do was move some of the multitudes of fish out in front of me to the beach, and then move my catch to the fish market. It looked pretty simple. The fish were right there, oblivious to all, ripe for the taking. There were no boats in sight to scare these swimming dollar bills. There were no surf fishermen to share the bounty. A nearly idyllic situation. What a story I was going to be able to tell—all those fish and how much I had made. (I was into that kind of bragging in those days.)

Out came the fiberglass pole with that well worn, reliable Penn Squidder reel which had seen so much service (and now, 40 years later is still serving). The lure pile yielded a sand eel look-alike and I was ready for the meat fisherman's dream. The first cast fell a little short, a small backlash shortened the cast. Backlashes develop when the reel overruns the outgoing line, a sure symptom of excitement and nervousness causing the "educated thumb" to forget to caress the reel at just the right time and with just the right pressure. Backlashes don't occur on today's spinning reels.

The backlash untangled, the nerves told to calm down, now I was ready. This was it, look out bass. The next cast went right along the edge of the shoal to a feeding school of big fish. Perfect placement. Now I was going to haul in one of those monsters. These fish were schooled, but they hadn't read the same script. They continued to feed undisturbed by my artful retrieve. Maybe, there weren't any fish in that particular spot at that particular time. This next cast will get one for sure, I thought. Again, the fish apparently didn't share my enthusiasm for going to market. Not one of the many lures in the lure box had the slightest attraction for any of those multitudes of linesiders. The light was fast fading, the fish still weren't biting. This was the time for sterner measures.

I rooted around in the back of the car, found a four foot piece of one-inch galvanized pipe, a large rusty screwdriver, and an assortment of bits of wire and twine. My visions of a successful trip to the fish market were rekindled. The screwdriver was lashed to the pipe and a primitive spear was born. Now you better look out fish. The back of the car was going to sag with the weight of those many fish. I was going to load up on those up-to-now elusive stripers. In the fast fading light, I waded out to the writhing mass of fish and bait and made ready to spear up a dozen or more. That "school" taught me something about a "bird in the hand," about the delightful contrariness of striped bass, and about my own inexperience when it came to fishing for what the experts call the Prince of Fishes. Those bass, almost as though they had a sense of humor, stayed just out of reach. I lunged at the bass I could almost touch. My clumsy efforts to spear these fish were a perfect counterpoint to the sleek elusiveness of these striped masters of the surf.

The sun dropped below the horizon and darkness set in. The sand eels darted here and there in their frantic efforts to escape being swallowed and the bass fed to their hearts content. The food chain was being played out right before my eyes, and I was not to be part of it—this time at least. It was a sight to behold, one that doesn't diminish with time, one that keeps me going back to the "school" of the ocean for more education, more sheer pleasure in the sights and sounds that attend a successful trip. Success, like the surf, comes in many shapes. The black and white of success in my early years (whether we got fish or not, and how many) is now all gray, tempered with the joy of being able to be there to see the sights and sounds of the multifaceted ocean. Today's success is an amalgam of what we see, what we hear, what we smell, and how it all fits together. If we catch a few fish, enough for dinner, so much the better, but today's success is not a matter of fish.

But the pursuit of fish is paramount to the trip. Without the excuse of being able to say, *"We're going down the bay to try for a bass for dinner,"* I don't think I would go very often. It still seems a trifle indulgent to this old Puritan to take a trip down to the water just to see the sun set over that magnificent Pleasant Bay, a sight to rival any natural phenomenon anywhere in the world. But if the purpose of the trip is to try for a fish for dinner, and the best spot happens to be where the sunset can be viewed in all its glory, we would now have the best of all possible worlds—food gathering and soul enriching pleasure combined. For me, success surely is being on this earth at this time, in this place, and being able to enjoy the many examples of nature's bounty so prominently and magnificently displayed.

For my generation, food gathering was the key to all our endeavors along the shore. It wasn't the "sport" of the hunt, it was the confidence that we could put food on the table—with our understanding of the location of the shellfish beds, of the movements of the schools of fish, of the most likely routes of the waterfowl. I suspect this need to put food on the table is one of the most basic of humankind. To be able to do this by our own efforts, with our own knowledge, satisfies a soul deep need. The usual alchemy of *effort = money = food* is reduced to the more basic, *effort = food*.

The fact that fresh game, be it fish, shellfish or ducks, tastes so very good also played and plays a big part in the harvest. Buying the same, somewhat aged, products has only a pallid resemblance to "the real thing."

As with any other education, learning the techniques of this food gathering is a challenging experience. For me it seemed as if the old-timers had all the luck and all the knowledge. They were often parsimonious, but more often generous about sharing it with us neophytes. Their good natured jibes, their references to our general ineptness were goads that spurred us on and made us want to do them one better. Eventually we did learn the "secrets" of their luck and came to realize this "luck" was knowledge coupled with practice.

Once learned, these skills were a gift of rare proportions. Getting a "mess" of something became practicing a skill, honing a technique until the difficult became easy—an athletic endeavor with a purpose, a mild adventure in the mild wild, effort with an immediate and tangible payback. The *all* surrounding waters of the Cape have always been nature's supermarket, providing nourishment for the body and enlightenment for the soul.

The ocean has been and is full of surprises. Big bass and big bluefish aren't the only denizens lurking in the depths. The teenage years were a time when bigness impressed us. We were down on the southern tip of Monomoy one evening hoping to snag a powerful bluefish or lunker bass out of Point Rip. It was a beautiful night, near dark, a perfect fishing time. A good sized moon was just making itself known.

A golden glimmer of light was flowing out of that heavenly body across the placid ocean in a narrowing band right to our feet.

Then out of nowhere, right in the wash, we spotted a pod of 10-to-12 foot long sharks in the golden moonlight. They were all but stranding themselves in the gentle surf. We could just make out the bait these enormous creatures had driven up on the shore. Schools of herring frenetically flapping, trying desperately to escape the onrushing maw of death. The baitfish were ribboning the beach in gently undulating strands of silver. The sharks were swimming parallel to the shore, mouths agape, scooping thousands of these small fish. For the little fish it was wholesale slaughter. For the sharks, it was an easy meal—shark hor d'oeuvres. For us on the beach, it was a spectacle of some magnitude. We had never seen sharks of this size. The little sand shark was common enough, but never anything like this. And there wasn't just one, there were at least half a dozen repeatedly semi-stranding and then, with the next wave, washing back out into the ocean. For a bit, we made a game of following the retreating wave, touching the half stranded shark, then running back up the beach. As we became bolder, we tried to grab a tail and pull the leviathan up on the beach. Ah, the optimism of youth. Sharkskin is easy to get a good grip on—no problem there. One problem was the shark weighed a ton plus, and together we weighed in at one tenth that. Another problem was that the shark was all muscle. Our muscle was mostly in our heads, thinking we could wrestle this creature up on the beach. With a disdainful flick of his tail he casually sent us head over teakettle tumbling across that moonlit watery beach. I doubt if that enormous creature ever knew we were there.

It was our first acquaintance with pure power, an awesome display of muscular might that far exceeded anything in our experience. But by flicking us off, the shark upped the stakes. Immediately, we wanted a shark, and obviously nothing we had on hand that night would do the trick. We plotted, we schemed and came up with a *plan*. The next evening we were ready. The *plan* entailed a harpoon, a long stout rope, and the spring steel bumper of the old Model A beach car. We'd harpoon the shark and the line would be attached to the middle of that springy bumper. We would play our fish with the car as a primitive fish pole and reel combined.

We were ready. Sure enough the next evening the sharks were at it again. It was time to put the *plan* in action.

Primal fear and sharks are synonymous. Something about those sleek, gray forms with that all-seeing and unblinking eye, sinuously gliding by, brings out deep-rooted, ancient fears that can turn the strongest resolve to putty.

It had all sounded so simple while we were making up the harpoon and rigging the line, getting ready. But standing at the edge of the ocean, what had seemed so simple became more ominous. We noted that the surf was not quite as benign as on the previous night and that the beautiful moon was mostly clouded over. Surprisingly too, the fish looked much bigger and remembering the almighty power in the casual flick of that tail, we thought maybe we ought to reconsider.

Those creatures seemed big enough to tow our old car out to sea. Losing the car would be bad enough, but if it happened in these circumstances we would lose the car, and worse, we'd never live it down. We didn't abandon our *plan*, however we did amend it. We added a knife and stationed Westy on the car's bumper to cut us loose if the car reached the water's edge. Now we were really ready.

One of us, harpoon in hand, rope trailing behind, was timorously approaching our quarry. About then an old rusted Jeep drove up to check out the goings on. A lone adult, a grizzled guy we'd never seen before, took one look at our elaborate preparations, and chuckled.

"You boys want one of those things? You expect to get one with that rig? Haw, Haw, Haw. I've got a shark getter right here. I'll get one of those dammed things for ya."

With that he rummaged around in the back of his Jeep, pulled out a rusty shotgun, chambered three shells, and walked down to the surf. He shot the next shark that wallowed up on the sand. The shark writhed violently, streaked out to sea and in a few minutes came out of the ocean at full bore, beaching itself in spectacular fashion. With both cars pulling we dragged this magnificent creature up on the high beach of Monomoy. He measured 12 1/2 feet long and was later identified by his teeth as a Great White Shark. Like the falling tide, the flush of the capture receded and a measure of sanity returned. That shark didn't belong on that beach, he belonged in the water. I think we were all somewhat ashamed of our "blood lust." All the rest of that summer, all that long glorious fall, that slowly disintegrating carcass was a vivid and odoriferous reminder of our folly. It was again one of those occasions when we asked ourselves "why" after the fact. We were learning more lessons.

Hunting In The Marsh

Shore fishing is seasonal, something we did only in the warm months of the year. Fall and winter brings a different kind of food to the table—flying food.

I've constantly been amazed by the evolution of thought that has been coursing through my soul over the years. Often what I considered "truth," the "gospel," has over time proven to be nothing more than an interesting sidebar on the way through life—no more "truth" than a first love always being an enduring love. Years ago, when I was just coming along, the idea of hunting seemed the height of maturity. I would never have believed that I would not always want to go hunting. My father, my uncles, most of their friends all hunted, even my mother hunted. Their generation hunted primarily to put delicious food on the table.

I couldn't wait for my 16th birthday when it would be my turn. The shells were cheap, the duck stamp inexpensive, and the ducks plentiful. The fact that the hunting itself was challenging fun was an added fillip that made the advent of November's hunting season eagerly anticipated. Oh, how I used to look forward to opening day. No longer. Now on opening day I cringe a little, as I listen to the carrumping of the guns out on the marsh and I wish the ducks well. No longer do I need to put food on the table, no longer are the stamps and the shells inexpensive, and no longer are the ducks plentiful, but I'll be willing to bet they still taste as good. Every fall, ducks that call Cape Cod home are in for a hazardous time. The hunters are out in force—the waterfowl, the black ducks, the sea ducks, and the geese had better watch out. Some of their kindred look-alikes scattered around the marsh, are just that, look-alikes. These decoys are anchored in front of some pretty fierce guns, manned by some pretty enthusiastic hunters. When I learned to fly, I was amazed how visible these duck blinds were from the air. What seemed invisible at marsh level was very visible, indeed obvious, from 200 feet up. I hope the blinds out on the marshes are as obvious to the ducks, as they were to me in a small plane. Thinking back to my own duck hunting days, I guess those blinds must have been obvious, as we sure didn't do much damage to any bird populations. Crouched, at age 16, in an ice sheathed blind one frosty morning, all eagerness and inexperience, I spotted a pair of ducks.

"Here they come!"

"Here they come!"

Jack, my father's long time hunting companion after a glance at the birds, offered this laconic reply: *" Yep, here they come, tail first."*

I looked a little more carefully before sounding the alert the next time.

I still remember my first gunning trip. A rite of passage like no other. One very early, very cold morning my father, my grandfather, and I set out for Pamet River 30 miles north of Chatham. All sorts of new experiences unfolded, I'd never been as far north as Truro and only rarely north of Chatham. The valleys were full of dense fog so the 30-mile trip was a roller-coaster ride—up in the clear, black, predawn darkness, then down in the dense milk-white, cloud filled valleys. It was a near magical happening and a wonderful prelude to this brand new adventure. In thinking back on it, I believe it was the only time the three generations, just the males, were alone together. It was a feeling of privilege, a delicious feeling of closeness. Me and the big guys. Maybe, just maybe, I was going to join their ranks, or at least get a leg up. This hunting business opened up all manner of wonderful possibilities. After arriving at the Pamet parking lot just before sun up, it was out to the flats to put out the decoys, and then up on the beach to hastily dig the blind that completed the setup. I was rationed to one shell at a time, and in view of my rank inexperience, it was a wise precaution. The three of us crouched low in the blind. As the sun came up behind us, the birds began to fly. The tolling of the decoys worked, sheldrake (mergansers) began to swing into range. We all let fly. The birds dropped, and what a top of the morning feeling that was. The crash of the guns, the jolt of the recoil against the shoulder, taking part in an adult ritual. I couldn't imagine life getting any better. That first trip, a psyche opener of the first rank, was the beginning of a few years of enjoyable hunting experiences and some delicious eating.

The Last Of A Kind

Firsts are greeted with much fanfare. Trumpets toot, drums drum, flags fly, all the trappings of an occasion. Not so with lasts. The last of a kind rarely draw much attention. They are just not there one day. One icy cold morning about 10 am, John Eldredge, a elderly neighbor from down the street, came rowing into the river just as we were setting out. His slow, measured strokes seemed a metronome of his life—a slow, measured life. He was in the same generation as my grandfather and had a son about my age. In his youth, he had been a market gunner. He had hunted game to sell, mostly ducks and geese. When there were plenty of waterfowl around that type of work provided income in a season when little else did. At any rate, this man was the only extant link with something I'd only read about. This plus the fact that he rode a bicycle when no one else his age did, lived in the only house in town without electricity, and had a working privy, made him in my eyes a figure out of the ordinary.

He had been anchored a mile or so off Harding's Beach in his flat-bottomed skiff with a string of shadows (wooden silhouettes of sea ducks) floating out behind the boat, waiting for the birds to swing by so he could get a shot. Now as he came rowing in the river with those slow, those very slow strokes, cold and wet, he looked tired to his soul. He landed a short distance away and just sat there nearly motionless hunched over the oars. He was rather aimlessly wiping his soggy mittens on his boots; every swipe left a sheen of moisture on the black boot top. He'd been sitting in an open boat on a very cold ocean for nearly four hours. He had rowed two miles each way. He was wet, and he was in his early eighties.

"I guess this will be my last gunning trip, I haven't got enough strength to hardly move."

He still had a two-mile bike ride home. As far as I know that was the last time this man, our only link with the market gunners, went out to ply a semblance of his former trade. No fanfare, no drums, just, no more. A measured acquiescence of age, done with acceptance and dignity and not a little private sadness.

As for me, my duck hunting experiences were all filled with fanfare. A new adventure around every corner. One unique experience was setting out the decoys in back of Strong Island on Pleasant Bay. Looking for a good place to hide, I all but fell in a sunken, half rotted hogshead (an enormous barrel) tucked under a bayberry bush. Someone, many years before had had the very same thought, at the very same spot. A nice connection with a kindred soul, a link with another time, another generation. I sure hope he had better luck than I did. The only duck I shot that day landed in a fairly tall pitch pine. I had to shuck boots and heavy jacket and, for a time, become one of the flying Wallenda's of the high wire act to retrieve the darn thing. Not many Cape Cod duck hunters shake their game out of trees.

Another eye opener was the time I was instructed to take an acquaintance of my father's on a sea duck shoot. As the older man shot, he let the birds drift away. He made no attempt to retrieve them. This seemed more than a little unusual to me and I said so.

"Why keep them?" he said. "You can't eat them."

"Then why shoot them?" I replied. It was a common belief, I later learned, that sea ducks were inedible. One of the off-Cape recipes for sea ducks entailed an oaken plank and the sea duck meat: the meat was supposed to be nailed to the plank and baked for six hours in a hot oven. Then the meat was to be thrown away and the plank eaten.

At the time, this was the first I ever heard of shooting something you wouldn't eat. It was also the first I had ever heard that these birds couldn't be eaten. My family had been eating them with *gusto* for generations.

The hunting phase of my life underwent a sea of change after a grim year halfway around the world. I was back on the Cape renewing my acquaintances with some of my old loves, the traditional Cape things of fishing, shellfishing and hunting. Fishing and shellfishing retained the same appeal. Hunting, however, had lost its lustre. On what turned out to be my last hunting trip, I held a dying duck in my hand. As I watched, it gasped out its life, and right then the images came flooding back. I came home from that trip and gave the guns away. I now look at the birds with compassion, as nature's gift to us, but do admit to an occasional desire to sit down to a duck dinner.

But even the dinners can have their surprises. Once while we were having a duck dinner someone asked for some stuffing. The server and all the others seated at the table were somewhat shaken to discover that the only stuffing available was the duck's own. In the haste to get the birds on the table, someone had forgotten to clean them. The memory of the astounded look on everyone's face when it was discovered that the birds hadn't been cleaned will not soon be forgotten, either. They still tasted very good, and in the memory banks, that taste lingers yet.

For the usual meals though, I can still see the plump, brown skinned birds steaming, three abreast on the milkstone platter, the rich, dark meat peeling off with each slice of the knife. I can most vividly recall the mouth-watering succulence of that moist red meat garnished with some Chatham oyster stuffing. I haven't had any wild duck for a long time, but the memories of that unique and so rich wild taste are to savor—my taste buds are ready.

But the times are changing. Of my three sons, only one has any interest in hunting, and I notice a slackening of this interest as he ages. What was once a way to put inexpensive food on the table is no longer. Duck hunting is now a luxury few can afford.

It is strange how the changing patterns of our lives move our viewpoints and our passions. I don't miss going hunting. I cannot think of anything that would entice me to go hunting. But all those memories are in color. They are rich vibrant colors with a life of their own.◆

Pat's Cats Have No Ears

⌒

Pat Cahoon lived down by Oyster River in one of the shanties along the shore. His was a hand-to-mouth existence. He lived by shellfishing—garnering the oysters, clams and quohogs so common along the river bottom. He was always dressed in cut off boots, the same well worn plaid shirt that was missing some buttons, and some shiny pants of uncertain ancestry. The ever-present pipe was shortened by years of use, and Pat seemed to shave on an uncertain schedule. He was one of those ageless people that go on forever looking about the same until one day you hear they are no longer with us.

Pat was of a time when that box with the flickering blue light wasn't keeping everyone home at night. His evening entertainment was to walk up to the local pub, the "Sou-Wester," and quaff a sudsy glass or two. If the shellfish harvest had been particularly bountiful, he would perhaps indulge more than was customary. On one of these occasions while wending his unsteady way back to the shanty, the need for a little rest overcame him. It was a cold winter's night, and Pat was wearing what had been fashionable 25 years earlier, a raccoon coat that probably had looked quite natty on the raccoons. As the fog of lassitude descended, he pulled the coat around him and lay down beside the little used road to dream fisherman's dreams.

Some time later when the town's only policeman was on his way home, the officer saw a hairy inert form on the roadside and stopped to move the "dead deer" out of the roadway. When he recognized the raccoon coat, he figured old Pat had been clipped by a hit and run driver. He flipped open the furry garment expecting the worst, and was greeted by:

"Come in and shut the door for God's sake, it's cold out there!"

Pat lived a simple life. When I knew him, his only companions were his animals.

"How is it that Pat's cats have no ears?" people would ask.

Pat lived with legions of felines. Nearly all of the older cats were bullet headed. They had no external ears, an odd circumstance and one that raised the obvious question. The cats' sleek appearance was caused by a gustatory overload of urea, according to one of my professors at the university. This substance is found in abundance in the body mass of scallops, the portion discarded in the cleaning process and the main diet of Pat's corps of cats every fall. Urea apparently causes a capillary breakdown, hence the lack of external ears. The lack of ears seemed to be the only thing untoward. This overload didn't impair the reproductive drive of these fecund felines. Their multitudes were slinking around the oyster shanties for years and undoubtedly their progeny are now spread far and wide.

Multitude Of Shellfish

As prolific as Pat's cats, Cape Cod's aquatic fields are harvested regularly by legions of eager eaters, animal and human. The shores of this watery peninsula are rich with shellfish beds, and no harvest is more anticipated than that of the bay scallop. As mentioned earlier, this bivalve is unique in that only the adductor muscle is eaten. The main body mass is discarded, or else the cats might not be the only ones with a streamlined appearance.

Scallops are big business. Not only are they delicious but when they are plentiful, many people make a substantial income from the harvest.

The first of October used to be opening day of the scallop season. Now it is November when the waters are a bit colder. October is the time for exploratory forays down to the sheltered waters of the rivers and bays, a time to take the drag, a glass bottomed bucket and a quahog rake and go look around.

If it is determined to be a good scallop year, this is also the time when the recreational and commercial fishermen get their gear in shape and make those glass bottomed buckets—devices that make spotting scallops a cinch, particularly in Cape Cod's windswept waters. They check their boats, their drags, and see if their tide charts are up to date. It's a lot like gardening. The "getting ready," the anticipation, is as much fun as the activity itself. In the planning, *every* scallop day is warm and windless, *every* weed bed is loaded with scallops, *every* drag comes in full. The fact that each year reality is considerably different does not dull the anticipation one whit. The committed recreational and commercial scallopers ready their drags, scoop-like devices made of a steel frame, chain, iron rings and netting, about three feet across, that are towed behind the boat. These drags ride along the bottom, gathering all in their maw — beer cans, mounds of seaweed, miscellaneous shells, an occasional befuddled flounder or blue crab, and with any luck, some scallops. Once in a bountiful year on Cape Cod Bay, my friend Warren Baker and I had the immense good fortune to strike a "hot spot." Our 36-inch drag, after much grunting and some cussing, came to the surface spilling over with large scallops after just a 10-minute tow. The drag held two and a half bushels. Four tows and a half hour later, we had our 10-bushel limit. Usually, scallops come much harder — a couple of buckets, sometimes as little as a couple dozen paltry scallops and mounds of seaweed and shells (shack) in a tow. The drag is always heavy to haul in. It is cold work sorting out the shack, and if only two dozen scallops are garnered, it is hardly worth the effort.

Scalloping is back-breaking work, but somehow it is fun, although I've never been quite able to figure out why. It's wet, it's cold, it's monotonous and it's expensive. Unless you scallop commercially, it is far cheaper to buy scallops, even at the current price of $12-a-pound.

Why then, with all these negatives, does anyone look forward to scallop season? But we all do, and when next the scallops "strike" in, my drag will be ready, the culling board freshly caulked. I'll be looking for someone to help pull in the drag and share the wet, cold joys of opening day. I can't explain the attraction, but it's there.

The boat work for all its wet, cold monotony is the fun part. The next part, opening the mountains of bivalves, is about as monotonous as can be imagined. All the time the scallops are coming over the gunnel the thought is lurking in the back of the mind: I've got to open these damn things sooner or later. It's a real push-pull of thoughts. The faster the gathering, the sooner the monotonous work of opening begins; the slower the gathering, the more time to savor the outdoors, but the opening will take longer into the night.

There are about 300 scallops in a bushel, five bushels to a limit. With plenty of practice you can open a bushel an hour. A really good opener has a shell in mid-air all the time. For most of us, it usually takes an hour and a half per bushel. A five-bushel limit is a lot of opening—drudgery with a capital "D." The saving grace is the yield, an average of eight pounds per bushel of the most delectable seafood that ever graced a table. If you are a commercial shellfisherman those eight pounds of meat will sell for a good hefty price. For the recreational fisherman, that same bounty will freeze well, eat well, and make dandy presents for friends.

The reason for all the effort in the gathering is the taste of these so very succulent, boneless bits of ambrosia. Scallops have a wonderful combination of salt and sweet that beggars description, and defies comparison. Try one, and you'll understand the phrase, "nectar of the gods." There are lots of savory meals that come out of the sea—the rich, full-bodied clam chowder, an oyster stew, a steaming, succulent lobster just out of the pot, a pile of red and steaming blue crabs heaped on a platter. But for exquisite taste, for the epitome of the treasures of the sea, I would nominate the bay scallop.

We cook scallops in two different ways and also eat them raw. Sautéed, they are excellent. However, you must be careful not to let the process overpower that delicate taste. Cook the scallops until they just lose their translucent look, not a nano-second longer. I occasionally roll them in flour or some type of breading, but only if I'm sure it won't interfere with the scallop's flavor.

Scallop stew. What a delight: a creamy, white, steaming stew, an errant white scallop or two slightly breaking the surface, swirls of yellow, melted butter patterning the hot liquid, and over all a sprinkle of nutmeg for color. Pavlov's dog has nothing on me. I can salivate just thinking about such a meal, especially on a cold winter's night with a fire in the fireplace. Then, all the work in the acquisition is forgotten. All that matters is that you are eating of the best—food you gathered and prepared from Cape Cod's rich pantry.

Of all the ways to eat scallops, my favorite is to eat them fresh, straight out of the shell. Sitting on the culling board, the panorama of the bay encircling you, the sun warming your bones, and having a few scallops to slide off the shell and down the throat... now there is some very special eating, eating that induces a wonderful feeling—a scallop high.

One of the many satisfying things about scalloping is the fact that the scallops we harvest are doomed anyway. They have spawned for the last time, and they will die in their third winter, whether we take them or not. The only time they are legal to take is when they are biologically defunct, a coincidence not shared by any other shellfish.

The first time my buddy Jim Eldredge and I were old enough to get a commercial license (at age 16), we did. This was going to be easy money and some darn good eating. I've mentioned how good scallops are right out of the water. Well, Jim and I were all *eager anticipation* on our first and only joint commercial shellfish venture. Over went the drags, the tow commenced and up came the drags with about two dozen scallops and two hundred pounds of seaweed and shells. The scallops stayed on the culling board, the seaweed and shells went back overboard, the drag went back for another try. The numbers of scallops per haul steadily declined. The *eager anticipation* gave way to the realization that 1947 was not going to be much of a year for scallops in Chatham. But all was not lost. We ate ourselves sick on the meager harvest. We may not have had enough to sell but we sure had enough scallops to eat. It was a warm fall day, the late afternoon sun full on our faces, the outboard was droning away, and the drags were wrinkling the few scallops out of their sanctuary in the eelgrass. Sitting on that muddy, seaweed-strewn culling board, Jim and I thought we had the world by the tail. Tomorrow was bound to be a better day and we were exactly where we wanted to be, doing exactly what we wanted to do.

Obviously, I have had a love affair with scallops ever since my dad suggested, "Try one of these." I love scallops, both in the gathering and in the eating. And it seems to be a shared obsession. Sane men who otherwise could easily afford to buy scallops will be out there opening day. They will be cold and wet, dirty and happy. Cape Cod craziness, soul satisfying succulence, whatever the reason, opening day will see an armada of ill assorted, ill equipped boats and an army of men, some women, plying the protected waters in hot pursuit of the wily scallop. I'll be right there among them.

Eating from the bounty of the land is a shared experience. The earliest peoples explored this land and stayed because food was so plentiful. Their shell heaps, middens, are still very much in evidence. Our methods of harvest are probably more efficient but the wild game surely tastes the same—delicious.

Pumpkin On The Pond

Shellfish are there for the taking, waterfowl on the other hand require a little more ingenuity. According to literature, one of the early methods of catching ducks involved pumpkins. In the early fall when ducks and geese were beginning to migrate, Indians hollowed out pumpkins and left them to drift around the Cape's ponds. In time, the waterfowl became used to these innocuous objects drifting around their feeding grounds at the whim of the wind. At that point the hunter cut out the bottom of the pumpkin, cut a few slits for eyeholes, inserted his head, and quietly swam out in the pond wearing the pumpkin. Swimming close to the unsuspecting birds, it was an easy matter to grab the quarry, to yank the birds under.

This scheme had a certain ingenious flair that in the reading proved irresistible. My friend Bob and I were in the "scuba" diving phase of our lives. We thought we would try a variation on the Indian's theme. One of the Station Ponds on Monomoy Point is fairly long, at least a quarter mile in length. Most days it harbors a goodly number of geese on its east end—birds that are usually just loafing during the daylight hours. Our plan was to don wet suits and scuba gear, head up the long pond underwater, and grab a couple of the unsuspecting birds. It should be easy, a piece of cake. This would be a high tech goose chase. We were 20th century Indians, and we didn't need the pumpkin ploy.

The 10-mile boat trip to the Point was uneventful. The lovely panorama of Nantucket Sound on the west and the undulating white sand dunes of Monomoy on the east made the boat ride, as always, a visual treat. Dragging the cumbersome and heavy wet suits, flippers and air tanks over the dunes and down to the pond's edge was a bit of a struggle, but there on the east end of the pond was the quarry. At least 20 of those fat geese were loafing in the water at the far end of the pond as usual, just idling the day away.

We donned our gear, the tight fitting suits, the awkward flippers, the overbalancing air tanks. We were ready for the great and revolutionary goose hunt. We had visions of fat geese, roasted brown and steaming and oozing oyster stuffing. We could all but taste them right there on the beach. All that remained was the quarter mile of open water that separated us from some delicious meals. No problem.

We slid into the water with all the stealth of any Indian, adjusted the multitudes of straps, air hoses, face masks and snorkels, and set off up the pond, one that we had seen a multitude of times but never had set foot or body in. From the shore, the water appeared clear blue, but it was pea soup in the pond. We couldn't find our way, and we had no compass. We should have quit right then. Finding the other end of the pond, and thereby the geese, was one of the essential prerequisites of our planned assault on goosedom. We were undeterred however, and swam blindly on. Visibility was about three feet, everything a bilious green, and we lost touch with each other almost immediately. Like the carrot in front of the donkey, the thoughts of that roasted and savory goose led us on. We also knew this method of hunting, if successful, would make getting the wary and elusive geese a snap. Geese on demand—G.O.D. for short.

On we went into the next hazard. Again unbeknownst to us, the pond bottom undulated wildly, 20-feet deep in one spot, two feet deep just beyond. This led to impromptu surfacings and splashings which, coupled with the lack of visibility, made for a markedly erratic and very obvious course up pond. We usually had no idea where we were and didn't know where the geese were either. We pressed on. Roast goose is a powerful lure. We'd made it, erratically to be sure, about halfway up the pond, but we noticed the geese had their necks elongated in a manner that said: "What's that?" or more than likely "What in hell is that?"

Our cover was blown. Underwater we went, further up the pond, another impromptu surfacing, more splashing and thrashing over the shallows, then down into the green depths again in a flurry of bubbles.

At the next strip of shallow water, we cautiously surfaced and *oh so* cautiously looked for another range on the geese. We had now about 150 feet to go. The geese were looking decidedly uneasy. Evolution hadn't prepared them for what they were seeing. Their necks were at extreme stretch. They all now faced into the wind, and this was not a good sign. Well, no matter, one more dive and we'd have them. Apparently the geese had had enough entertainment for the day. When we surfaced after a lengthy and fruitless underwater search for paddling feet, our quarry was nowhere to be seen—just a few feathers drifting around to mark their departure point. Visions of that succulent roast goose flew off with them, replaced by the thought of that long swim back up the pond. At least on this trip we didn't need stealth. We splashed our way up the pond, and in doing so learned that geese have a sense of humor. Resting, loafing really, all the geese we had focused so much energy on were now in the exact spot on the pond's edge where we had begun the adventure. Two of the cussed things were actually standing on our dry clothes. Startled geese often lighten the load for a hurried takeoff. These two were no exceptions. Not only did we not get any geese, we had two shirts to clean. Our high tech pursuit had disintegrated into ignominy of the most vile kind. As the geese flew over us for one last look I'm sure I heard salvos of goose laughter coming down from on high. We deserved it and we chuckled a little at ourselves, but not for long. We both started to scratch, some unexplained itch was taking over our bodies. In less than an hour, large red welts were all but covering our bodies, and how they itched. A few hours later we were in constant motion and about ready to hire an extra scratcher or two. That's when I vaguely remembered from a dusty Parasitology course something about a parasitic life form that is called "Clam Digger's Itch." That's what we had. It's not in any way harmful. It disappears in two or three days, but itches every minute of the duration—more goose laughter, if only they had known. We would like to have been able to let the geese know they were welcome to Station Pond, but on reflection I guess they already knew that. We were the ones that needed to know that Station Pond is for geese, not high tech goose-getters.

Off The Shores Of Monomoy

Monomoy is also the seasonal domain of the aquatic mammals. The great whales pass by on their way to Stellwagen Banks up off Provincetown. Their smaller more graceful cousins, the dolphins, were once fairly common off Monomoy's shores. The rich feeding grounds nourish and hold these sleek creatures in the island's watery pastures for a time.

Each year, they typically grace the nearshore waters of Cape Cod with their sinuous, leaping pursuit of food. They often, seemingly just for the fun of it, ride the bow wave of any boat they fancy. Passengers thrill to the graceful antics of these sleek, beautiful creatures that seem the epitome of marine design. Sailing in Nantucket Sound was once a near guarantee that sooner or later the bow wave would have more than water in it. Those black and white six-foot long, smiling, bow riders would be whooshing just off the bow of our old catboat bringing exclamations to our lips and wonder to our eyes. For the dolphins, it must have been tame sport. The old catboat rarely exceeded five knots and these magnificent animals can easily keep up with a twenty-knot boat. Maybe they, too, wanted some company out there in that broad expanse of water and figured that slow as we were, we were better than nothing. Perhaps they were looking at us and wondering why we chose to slog along at such a slow speed when they could easily go four times as fast. Maybe they wanted us to join them. I would have liked to. These boisterous animals seem to have a wonderful time zooming through the water, looking at life with those intelligent eyes. Eyes are the window to the soul, anyone who has ever looked a dolphin in the eye probably yearns to bridge the gap to that intelligence.

Occasionally, we used to see these mammals flashing by Monomoy's east side. Monomoy was where I saw my first dolphin near at hand. There is a sand bar half way down the east side of Monomoy. It is a long bar arching towards the northeast, the landward terminus of the fearsome Chatham Bars. This bar acts like a giant fish trap, and as such, is a likely place to look for a bass or two. While doing just that one glorious August morning, we saw a shark fin a short distance off the beach. With teenage excitement at fever pitch, we cast every lure we had at that fin, tried every trick we knew. All to no avail. The fin kept cruising back and forth, back and forth, just off the beach, not even slightly interested in our offerings. Nothing dulls desire more than being ignored. We soon gave up our quest for a hooked shark and moved on down the beach to more promising piscatorial pursuits at Point Rip.

The Cape's maritime waters are some of the worst on the Atlantic Coast and the sea has harsh punishment for the inexperienced and unlucky. One of the deep-rooted apprehensions of most of us young beach-goers was what we would do if we chanced upon a body on the beach. We figured with the number of boats lost each year, a body or two was likely to wash up on the beach and we were on the beach all the time, sooner or later we were bound to coincide. Talking about this possibility one night at the camp, my father dryly opinioned that a local seedy character, Jake, would probably first go through the pockets, then report it. On a more basic level, we all wondered how we would mentally handle discovering a body on the beach—the morbid anticipations of youth.

We were coming back from Point Rip on the low tide. Beach driving was at its best at low tide. The broad, flat, hardpacked sand provided easy going for the old flivvers we drove. We could coax them up to the dizzying speed of about 25 or 30 miles-an-hour, and revel in that heady feeling. It was a carefree run up the beach on that lovely warm day, with bright sunshine and good friends.

We cruised over the gentle undulations of the beach, heading back to the camp and lunch. But on this beautiful day, this "all is right with the world day," things took a sudden turn. What we all had wondered about, one of our more morbid thoughts, was gently rolling in the surf right in front of us. We saw the round shape, the arm flopping back and forth in the wash. This was *it!* We came upon the body quite suddenly. We were going at flank speed and none of our old cars had any semblance of brakes. Our apprehension was overruled by momentum. We coasted up next to the cadaver and to our immense relief discovered that the "body"—"the shark" of the morning—was one of those flawlessly designed dolphins, dead on the beach. The "arm" of our imagination was one of its fins. This handsome creature was about six-feet long. There were no wounds. No disfigurement. No reason for it to be up on the beach.

One among us, Ed, was a pre-med student, and so we *had* to tow the carcass off the ocean beach, across the dunes, back to the camp for some dissection practice. The thought of that lithe body just rotting on the beach, and the following thought that perhaps we could find the cause of death was the stimulus for the desecration—that and a touch of heightened macabre curiosity that all young people seem to have in abundance. Obligingly, one of Nantucket Sound's sandbars was dry on the low tide, a perfect place for the autopsy. The rising tide would wash away the gore. By the time Ed made the first cut, he had garnered quite an audience (by Monomoy standards). At least half a dozen of us were looking at the goings on—the whetted knife, the sleek, smooth body. It seemed a shame to desecrate such a perfect shape.

The cause of death and the aimless back and forth movements we had noticed that morning were immediately apparent. The poor thing was trying to deliver a baby and had died in the attempt. The perfectly formed young animal was in the breech position and impossible to deliver. What a shame. Two such beautiful animals, dead on the beach. It was only later that I learned that nature has little tolerance for mistakes. That day, on that sandbar it seemed like such a waste of perfection. After the quick solution to the puzzlement of the cause of death, Ed started the autopsy in earnest, pulling out yards of intestines, commenting on the heart, the lungs and the similarities to us humans. I don't think Ed, in his single-minded pursuit of knowledge, ever noticed that his audience had melted away. We, too, had noticed the similarities to humans, the oceans of red blood, the split rib cage, open and gaping at the sky, and that human-sized heart. As the dissection proceeded, the similarities to ourselves became more and more obvious, and the audience less and less so.

We timorous neophytes of anatomy retreated to a nearby dune to contemplate the peaceful horizon, the azure blue sky, the white puffy clouds, the blue waters, and the white sands of Monomoy. They seemed a welcome and soothing contrast to the bloody goings on out on the flats. Life has some bumpy spots, and the dunes of Monomoy have always offered the same solace.◆

Part II

The Camp On Monomoy

⌒

The name *Monomoy* is about all that remains of the native American heritage in this corner of the Cape—probably a bastardized word for the group of natives living in this area, the Monomoyicks. The town of Chatham was originally called Monomoyick; now just the island carries this proud native heritage, eminently fitting because only the island retains the tranquil wild beauty of the early times. The town itself is lovely, but much of its wild beauty has long since given way to our desire to conquer the land.

Monomoy and its surrounding shoals played a pivotal bit part in the founding of this nation. Were it not for the providential appearance of a summer wind in November, the Pilgrims would have perished on Monomoy's outriding shoals. These dangerous shoals acted as a barrier to the *Mayflower's* southward journey, turning the vessel north to Provincetown and then on to Plymouth. The *Mayflower*—with her 12-foot draft, laden with one hundred souls, low on water, with no firewood left—was headed for certain doom on Monomoy's shoals. One of the Cape's vigorous northeast winds pushed her down on what is now called the Broken Part of Pollock Rip, down to water much shallower than the *Mayflower's* draft. Captain Christopher Jones saw breaking water ahead and to the east, Monomoy on his west and thought all was lost. But such was not to be. An unusual wind for that time of year, a summer southwesterly came roaring over the horizon at the last possible moment—the only wind that could spring the trap they were in. Perhaps it was a reward to this stalwart group of religious pioneers. With sails aback, the good captain turned his sluggish ship out of the dangerously shoal waters, jogged around off Provincetown all night and anchored in Provincetown's deep harbor on November 10. Eventually they settled some weeks later in what is now Plymouth, rather than their original destination, the Hudson River area.

While the stalwart Captain Jones saw Monomoy as only one side of a three sided trap, most of us privileged to see this island have seen it for its splendors. My family's association with this lovely sandy peninsula is long, at least 350 years. My direct ancestor William Nickerson's purchase of Chatham in 1640, included Monomoy. Almost 200 years later, my great-grandfather Eldridge bought some 500 acres of "beach and meadow" at Inward Point just after the Civil War—bought it for $10. My father's brother put together a tiny camp on the island in the late 1920's, and my father bought another beach camp for $30 just after the war.

Prior to that, we had stayed in borrowed camps on Monomoy, mostly Doc Keene's sturdy, tight camp at Inward Point. The camp my folks eventually bought was close enough to the obliging Keenes that we always shared the common outhouse. My earliest memories of the island are in the Keene's camp, their old cast iron stove roaring away as it pumped out the heat, driving off the chill of a November evening. Monomoy has always been a integral part of my being, a lodestone of my life. Monomoy's sand is forever in my shoes.

By a major stroke of luck and the great generosity of my uncle Dick, I was given in my teenage years the use of his long unused beach camp on family land at Inward Point, about half way down Monomoy.

The camp had started its beach existence in the late 1920's when Monomoy was then a 10-mile long, white sand peninsula. Over the years a hot dog stand, a bombing target's bullseye, a wrecked boat's deck, and a hunter's sink box were all incorporated into the "camp." The building, originally my grandfather's chicken house, was flaked, taken apart in sections, and moved by my uncle five miles down Monomoy. A very rudimentary foundation was leveled up and the sections were re-erected quickly. A camp was born. It was a modest enough camp measuring only 8 foot by 12 foot, smelling faintly of chicken on the wet days.

The Bunk Room

A small hot dog stand in Chatham went out of business in the 30's;

the small building, not much more than a lean-to, had to be removed. The camp needed a bunk room. No matter how friendly two people are, an 8 foot by 12 foot camp is pretty tight going. The hot dog stand was also flaked, carted out to Inward Point, then resurrected against the east end of the camp. A suitable opening was made, and the camp had a bunk room. At this point the place became more real. No longer a wooden tent, it now boasted a stove, a pump, a table, and a bunk room.

The shanty was used as a gunning camp, a fishing camp, a trysting camp, but mostly it was a great place for young people to get together to hatch young people's schemes away from the more censorious eyes of the older generations.

World War II put a stop to beach excursions. Deserted, the camp's windows were broken, the door cannibalized for another camp, the stove taken and the pump removed until all that remained was a shell of the original structure. With no windows or doors, the restless winds of Monomoy soon partially filled the camp with sand, thus setting the stage for the next act in the camp's sheltering ways.

In a human sense, the camp was a pretty desolate place, but it didn't lack for occupants. An occasional skunk or raccoon wandered in for shelter. Food was scarce, so they moved on. Deer huddled in the lee of the place during the winter's howling storms. The mouse population, though, flourished. These were the graceful little deer mice with long tails, big ears, tan backs, and white bellies. Bayberries and grass seeds provided food in abundance, and the camp's sheltering structure kept the patrolling hawks and owls at bay.

Other graceful though more seasonal users of the camp, were the swallows—those trim, colorful, aerobatic, insect eating birds. Again, the camp supplied the missing ingredient: shelter. The eaves of the old place provided ample shelter and support for all the swallow nests they would hold. The swallow's swooping flight added a touch of grace to the otherwise bleak looking structure that appeared to be slowly settling in the beach.

Plant life was also moving in. Poison ivy, which seems to thrive on what appears to be sterile sand, found the camp's structure much to its liking. Tendrils crept up under the shingles, through the windows, up the eaves, and eventually encapsulated the place in a green shroud. The tough beach grass moved right up to the ivied shingles, locked in the shifting sands, and it too prospered. In short, the camp was a going concern, sheltering, as always, those that came to it. It was also gradually being buried by the mobile sands of Monomoy.

I was given the use of this beach camp for about fifteen years, at a time in my life in the 1950s when better solace for a troubled mind could not have been imagined.

A Trip In The Dory

Pete Hartley was a good friend and the closest thing I've ever had to a brother. He was a few years older than I, but not enough older that we didn't scheme and plan to ensnare each other's girl friends. Pete was wildly impractical. I was fairly practical. Pete was erudite. I was not. But what we both shared was a passionate love for Monomoy and all it entailed. In other words we got along just fine. At a time in our lives when we both needed a major project (both of Pete's parents had died suddenly, I was just back from a grim year in Korea), the renovation of the beach camp was something we could both attack with need and gusto but with very little money.

We shoveled the camp out, jacked the little place up a couple of feet, replaced the rotted boards, resurrected another rudimentary foundation, leveled it up, and fought the poison ivy to an uneasy truce. Another stove (an old Glenwood, a beauty) was found, the pump and sink replaced, the windows re-glazed, a new door built, and the camp was humming once again. I was amazed then and I am still amazed at the generosity of people. In the rebuilding of this tiny shanty casual acquaintances would stop us and ask, *"You guys need a pump?"* or *"I know of a stove if you want to pick it up."* Most of the equipment in the camp came to us in this casually generous way.

The camp needed everything that makes a structure livable, and as we were both college bound what the camp needed had to be gleaned from any source. We were into recycling long before it became popular. Anything free, and we were first in line.

We moved fast when offered a couch. Couches aren't made for floating or boating. Pete and I unwittingly discovered this fact one cold, blustery day in May. We met the couch-givers at their home which fortunately was only a short distance from the harbor's edge. The overstuffed monster was in fair shape, but what we hadn't realized was the size of this mini-monolith. It was nine-feet long. The longest dimension in the camp was only 12 feet and there was a door in that wall. After a hurried consultation, we took the couch anyway. It was free, and it was in fairly good condition, and we could always cut it down to size somehow. It was all we could do to move the thing, but we did manage, after a struggle, to lash it on top of one of our cars. A nine-foot couch upside down on an 11-foot car is not the stuff of aerodynamics, but it certainly causes a number of stares. The people who gave us the monster were shaking their heads as we drove away. Cars passing had heads popping out the windows. Hikers stopped in their tracks to watch the giant upside down couch proceed majestically towards the harbor.

Aside from the unwieldy look of the thing, the move was uneventful and the couch got a good airing. We wrestled the monster off the car and to the harbor's edge. We then ran head on into an unexpected problem. Pete's boat was a 16-foot dory. Dories are good boats, for their purpose there are none better. They will take almost any sea with aplomb and unlike most boats, dories do better with a load aboard. Part of this sea-kindliness is due to their modified wedge shape. The deeper they are loaded, the more stable they become. That is if they are loaded from the bottom up, with the weight low as the designer intended.

This ungainly couch was too wide to fit within the confines of the dory, the only way we could get it aboard at all was to perch it on the gunwales. The load was much too unbalanced to put it sideways across the boat. It seemed best to load the nine-foot length of the monster lengthwise, but this was none too good. Two problems immediately surfaced: the couch was too big and heavy; no room for the passengers. The rake (slant) of a dory's stem and stern was such that the boat had only 10 feet of bottom. With the nine-foot couch aboard, that left six inches on each end of the craft for us. We solved both of these problems by putting ourselves under the couch. That put some weight down low where it belonged, made the boat more stable, and gave us room to make the move but not much room to move. We would have to make the trip on our knees but this was a minor inconvenience. This kneeling position had the added advantage of being a good praying posture, but this aspect didn't occur to us until we were two or three miles offshore and halfway to the island and sinking. The sheer (curve) of the gunwales meant the load was only hitting the boat near each end, leaving quite a gap in the middle of the craft. There was room enough for us to wriggle under the couch and into the waiting maw of the boat, and space to look out either side. We were totally blind forward. This wasn't the boating season so there was little likelihood of collisions. We knew the way, we really didn't need to see forward.

Another aspect of dory design that should be mentioned is the extreme narrowness of each end of the boat. Again, this makes it sea-kindly when rowed, when the weight is down low in the middle where the oarsman would sit. In our wisdom (after all, we were children of the mechanical age), we had cut a well in Pete's dory's stern to fit an outboard motor. In our haste to save ourselves some rowing, we totally overlooked the fact that dories were never designed to have weight in either end, and that outboards are heavy, as is the person operating the motor. That outboard motor well became the Achilles heel of Pete's dory, on this trip and forever after.

We rigged a stick to the motor so we could steer from under the load, fired up the engine, and set off for the camp at Inward Point, five miles across Nantucket Sound. The trip out of Stage Harbor was uneventful. To any onlookers the sight was an odd one—a top heavy dory swaying and lurching its way out of the harbor, with apparently no one on board. A fellow I talked to later said he had seen us crossing the harbor and for a short while thought he was seeing a boat that had escaped the driver.

Once out of the harbor's protected waters, things took a turn for the worse. The northwest wind was stirring up some small waves, and the further we got from the shelter of Hardings Beach, the bigger the waves became. It wasn't long before we noticed a little water sloshing around the bottom of the boat. Did we have a leak? Where was that water coming from? We still had three and a half miles to go, and this was decidedly not the season to go swimming.

The reason outboard boats have wide sterns is twofold. The width gives the boat a large planing surface and at the same time counteracts the tendency of these motors to pull the stern down in the water. Dories, as mentioned, have narrow sterns. They can't overcome this pull-down tendency at all. While pushing the boat ahead, that work-saving motor was also pulling the stern down,

down deep enough to allow water to lap over the newly cut-in well. Not much, just a cupful at a time. But each cupful invited more aboard, and pretty soon the cupfuls would be inviting quarts on the way to gallons, then barrels, then we and the couch would be swimming in this very cold water.

This was not good. We were kneeling in icy water that was very slowly getting deeper. And as waves were getting bigger, we were sinking faster. At the present rate of submergence, we were not going to make it to the beckoning shore. Pete slowed the motor, which in turn slowed, but didn't stop, the intake of water. I took off one of my boots and started bailing, not an easy thing to do, on your knees under a couch, but with survival at stake, it was doable. I couldn't quite keep up with the inflow, but the scales of whether or not we would make it or not, seemed to tilt a little more in our favor. The cold water was nearly up to our waists (as we were kneeling) when the dory gave a gentle sigh and settled to the bottom in two feet of water just off the camp. It had been an exciting trip, with disaster narrowly averted. We had no life preservers nor did we see another boat. On the other hand, we were teenagers and all teenagers know they are indestructible and therefore they don't worry. We were soaked, but the couch and the outboard had survived the trip in fine shape, and of the three, we would dry out the easiest and fastest. All in all, a successful trip.

After manhandling the monster mound off the boat, across the beach, up over the dune and down to the little snuggled in camp, our real work began. We had to remove the door frame to get the cumbersome couch in the camp, and once in, as expected, it wouldn't fit anywhere without some serious modifications to both the camp and the sofa. The surgery was primitive and fast — two bookshelves removed, and a foot of length cut off the monster.

That couch supported us in comfort for many years. But never did Pete or I sit or sleep on it without the memories coming to mind of that sinking trip across Nantucket Sound, crouched under the couch, bailing with a boot, and willing the shore closer.

The couch was just one of the fixtures the camp needed. In my mind, no camp was complete without a lookout tower. The little camp was a half mile or so from the nearest hot spot for bass, Schooner Bar. From a lookout tower, we would be able to see across the island for any activity, bird or human at the bar, and know to get over there for a try at those linesiders. And as often happened in the rebuilding effort, as if anticipating our needs, the beach provided the raw materials for the project. On one of our scouting expeditions, we came across a ruggedly built set of stairs complete with hangers washed up on the outer beach. Those stairs, plus three washed up weir poles and a few pieces of planking, gave us a superior tower, one that on a clear day we could see as forever as we wished. What a fine view it was. I can still "see" from that shaky but surprisingly resilient two-tier tower.

At this point, beach access was relatively easy. It was just a short row across Stage Harbor to the little hollow by the Coast Guard boathouse where we kept our beach cars. Easier access meant more traffic, and more traffic meant more accumulation of stuff. The little camp was bulging at the seams. The same limitations of two decades before were in force—where to put the people and the accumulating junk that lurked around the place. We needed a bigger camp, and had no money to spend on such luxuries. The beach and a little patience once again provided the solution.

The bulls-eye of the old bombing target in Monomoy's midsection was rotting into the sand. Its frame provided a low cost solution to an addition to the camp. Enough of this wood was salvaged to double the size of the camp. Some attractive, turn of the century, hard pine interior paneling was scrounged from a partially demolished camp at the Powder Hole, four miles down the beach to finish off the interior. By the time all these alterations and additions were completed, the camp was really quite comfortable. It now boasted a couch, a table and chairs, and most everything in it had just one use. No more table converting into a back rest and in a tight situation converting to a bed. Now the table was a table. It even had its own homemade drawer with odds and ends of silverware in it.

The camp really needed some nice cedar shingles to finish off the outside. Again Monomoy's larder supplied the materials. The winter winds had finally flattened a long abandoned Coast Guard barn at what had always been called the Middle Station. The collapsed building was sheathed with lovely cedar shingles painted white. Again, need and supply were close at hand. The shingles were popped off with a long handled spade, turned over painted side down to serve again. A discerning viewer might notice a white butt or two, but the shingles looked very nice, ready to shield the camp for another 20 or 30 years.

The camp now was both trim and tidy on the outside, but on the inside it was slowly filling up. Doubling the size of the camp seemed through some alchemy to quadruple the amount of stuff we were saving: axes, saws, car parts, bits of boats—all under the couch, in the stove, under the bunks. Every nook and cranny filled with stuff too good to throw away and not quite good enough to keep. We kept it anyway, 'just in case'.

The catalyst for a solution to this crowding came when we were driven from the camp by a horribly smoking stove. Pete, for lack of space, had put an extra pair of old sneakers in the oven and had forgotten about them. Roasted rubber invites action, usually retreat. Storage was too tight—not enough room for all the treasures we weren't about to throw away.

About this time some hunter's sink boxes (heavily built, watertight boxes about five-foot square) were showing up along the outer beach after being buried for years. These were left over from the 1920's when Monomoy played host to tens of thousands of ducks and a few hunting clubs. Most of these boxes were broken up by the encroaching surf, their pieces scattered along the shore. One box, tougher than the rest, survived the surf's battering ways, and washed up on the upper beach intact. Again, as so often before, a timely supply matched an obvious need—a storage room.

The sink box was skidded to the camp and stood on end. The camp's eaves were extended, more shingles were gathered and attached, a door was put on and that was the last time that box was empty.

The camp was really taking shape now—main room, bunk room and storage shed, all shingled and tight. The next supply presented itself before we realized we needed it.

Some years previously, a 40-foot Novi fishing boat, the "I Am Alone", had grounded and broken up on Monomoy Point. The heavily built deck washed up on high beach intact. Pete, thought this deck would make a dandy front porch for the camp, and he was right, it did—a rather plebeian use for a boat builder's art, but a use at that. At least it wouldn't rot into the sand unnoticed. A great deal of effort and laughter over the next two days moved this nail studded, waterlogged unwieldy piece of boat to its next and final resting place. Boat deck to front porch.

The camp was as complete as it would ever be. It seemed to snuggle down in the dunes, sheltered from the winter blasts of Arctic air by the high dune to the north, but open to the usually gentle cooling south winds of summer.

The modifications weren't very costly, mostly the beach provided all that was necessary. The work, (sure it was work) and all the effort that went into making the camp didn't seem like work. It was making something from nothing—challenging fun. Good Cape Cod fun.

Enjoyment. Well, the camp provided that in abundance. Now years after its demise, it's still providing enjoyment in the retelling—memories of freshly caught bluefish filleted and broiled over the coals., memories of steamers dug from nearby Hospital Creek and cooking on the old Glenwood. The lengthy wait, then the volcanic rush of steam pushing the lid off the old dented kettle, sending a salty aromatic gush of salt steam to mushroom across the ceiling. Three boil-overs like that and the clams were ready and the old stove had a further patina of white salt crystals accenting its black top.

The camp's very existence added a richness to any meal. Tastes were magnified, hungers were heightened and meals—sometimes slap dash, sometimes thought out—were always delicious.

The camp seemed to tick along in an aura of contented happiness, doing what it had always done, providing shelter for its occupants. The laughter and the good times seemed to fuel the fortunes of the camp. No thought was ever given that this little oasis of happiness wouldn't always be there.◆

Surrounded By Water

Cars were always a major part of the pleasure of life on Monomoy.

The word island means *surrounded* by water, and Monomoy is no exception. Stage Harbor, for us, was a moat of some magnitude. Cars had to be floated across the harbor on oyster scows—floating platforms supported by two airtight pontoons and propelled by a small outboard motor. These unusual craft were ideal for their designed task and for ferrying cars across the harbor. For the price of $5, a barge would take a car across to its final resting place. Very few cars ever came back. Once on the island, there they stayed and are there still.

These scows were well suited for the task of car carrying, but were working near the limit of their load capacity. I happened to be at the edge of the harbor one day when a heavily built, military surplus, four-wheel drive truck was being ferried across. Whoever owned this massive truck had built a primitive camper rig on the bed. It was big, unwieldy and heavy, just the opposite of the stripped down cars we were using. The loaded scow was just at water level. A short distance from shore it looked as if the truck was somehow sitting on the water. The scow was invisible. All went well until the midpoint of the harbor. Then the truck's owner (somebody from off Cape) decided for some reason to go to the bow of the scow. His weight was just enough to start the heavily laden, slow moving barge on a slight downward slant. The scow's owner yelled to the other fellow to get back fast but he didn't move fast enough. The scow motor was reversed, but it wasn't powerful enough to counteract the weight of that massive truck and the forces of gravity. Slowly, inexorably, the barge with its heavy load slid under the calm, cold waters of Stage Harbor until all that was left on the surface were two bellowing men. One bellowing for help, the other raining curses on his fellow swimmer. On shore, the half a dozen of us could scarcely believe what we'd just seen. But when the shock wore off, laughter was close behind. Someone took a nearby skiff and towed the two soggy souls ashore. We chuckled for a long time to come. It isn't every day that Stage Harbor plays host to a car sinking—boats now and then, but cars going down were quite unusual.

Apparently the scow didn't like the bottom of the harbor, and decided to shuck its too cumbersome load. It bobbed up with the drowned outboard motor, now adorned with seaweed, still attached. The huge truck was later dragged out of the harbor mud and up on the shore like some prehistoric monolithic monster— sporting splintered wood, soggy mattresses and blankets, smashed windshield, and crumpled fenders. It was oozing the muck of the ages out of every crack and crevice, and looking as woebegone as any vehicle could. While workers hosed it down, a small but legal sized lobster and half a dozen crabs washed out of the crevices. Charley, a local wit and one of the onlookers, happened to be stand- ing next to the truck's owner,

"Around here fella, we usually just sets pots for lobsters."

But this was the exception, not the norm. The trip across the harbor almost always went without a hitch. This is not to say we didn't all breath a sigh of relief when the soft tires of the old cars rolled onto the shores of Monomoy.

Once the cars were on the island there were few restrictions, other than those imposed by gasoline and common sense. We usu- ally had plenty of gasoline; common sense, on the other hand, was often in short supply. Monomoy's isolation and our own lack of cash spawned ingenuity. If we wanted something we made it. If we broke something, we fixed it. Monomoy was a sandy campus where failure usually meant a long weary walk off the beach.

Car repairs figured high on our list of things that needed doing. All of the cars we had on the beach had lived a long and arduous life on the mainland, and then were consigned to the junk yard. I never heard of anyone paying more than $75 for a beach car. That was a stratospheric price. The way I acquired an old 1938 Chevy two door was not unusual. The owner offered it for $10, if we could get it running. If not, I could have it for free. It cost me nothing.

Buying worn-out cars and putting them in one of the most demanding environments imaginable meant we spent a lot of time *in* and *under* cars. I remember Pete and I one day replacing a worn out, vital part on one of his much loved Model A's. We were doing elementary surgery on the handy oil changing ramp behind the abandoned Coast Guard station on the top of Bean Hill (so named for the Coast Guard cook's proclivity for low cost meals). As we happily became grease-covered, we became aware of a discordant sound that soon resolved itself into an old black Studebaker sedan laboring its way up the steep hill. Loaded to the gunwales with all manner of people, it was quite a sight. We had never seen any such vehicle on Monomoy before. Fords were the preeminent car of choice. Hard experience had taught us that lesson many times over. Occasionally, one of us would get a Dodge or Chevrolet over on the island, but those were invariably lesser cars. They just didn't stand up to the vast amount of ill treatment that was to be their lot. For some reason, Fords tolerated the seemingly intolerable — the relentless diet of salt air, salt water, sand, neglect and whatever else we kids and nature threw at them. But that Studebaker was an unknown quality about to endure a testing the automotive engineers, in their wildest nightmares, never envisioned. And from the looks of things, all was not well. Bean Hill was merely the first obstacle in a long series of hurdles ahead of this obviously tired car. Things didn't look good. Steam was gushing out of every crack and crevice. These were not tendrils of steam, but solid, heavy, gouting steam — steam that presaged an imminent and metal-cracking end. This was not a good sign.

Another woeful omen: the sagging car was sitting very low on its springs, dragging and scrapping its way along the deeply rutted road. Ahead the ruts were much deeper. Most ominous of all though, was the song of the engine, a song that was pitiful in the extreme. The sound now issuing from the depths of this faltering car was a wavering wail of metallic anguish telling us that maybe the fat lady was singing and the aria was nearly over.

They went over the hill and down the ruts to the open beach. We went back to our project. As we laboriously replaced the rust encrusted bits and pieces of the car, the sun rode across the heavens. It was a lovely day, bright sun, moderate temperatures. One of those typical Cape Cod summer days that you hope will go on forever. When the last bolt was fastened, the last nut tightened, a test ride was in order. So it was down that same Coast Guard Hill and out on the open beach and right there at the bottom of the hill, right where the glacial moraine melded into open beach, was evidence of doom.

The old Studebaker was in the classic posture of woeful car. Both sides of the hood were up baring that defunct engine to the sky. Tendrils of smoke were, like departing spirits, coiling up from the non-responsive metal. Silence pervaded the immediate area like a funeral shroud.

Off on a nearby dune, the passengers were more or less arrayed in beach party fashion. They were making the best of the situation. The blankets were spread, people were eating and drinking, kids were racing around having a high old time. Except for their centerpiece, that black Studebaker, it was typical beach party.

We recognized the car's disgusted owner, and asked if we could help. He wondered if we could take the people back to the boat at the edge of Stage Harbor a mile or so distant. That we could easily do, and did in a couple of fast trips. We left the owner and his gang at the harbor's edge. After he thanked us for the taxi job, he asked how much change we had in our pockets. It seemed like a strange request but we rooted around and came up with 29 cents. The owner, a man named Ralph, took one look at our change, took it in his hand and handed me the key to the carcass back on the beach. "Sold! If you want it, it's yours." We hurried back to our unexpected purchase, circled it a couple of times but could find no redeeming features. Most of the cars we drove had died at least once and been resurrected, but this one was far deader than most of the cars we had ever seen. Too dead perhaps to wake up for another life.

We drained five or six gallons of gas out of the tank, poured most of this into our tank, and sloshed the rest over the forlorn heap and touched her off. It was a magnificent conflagration, red flames and billowing black smoke.

The frame sat there for a year or two and then the shifting sands of Monomoy slowly covered the rusty wreck. Some years later a new opening into Nantucket Sound broke through Monomoy just south of Morris Island. One of the navigational hazards of this new opening was a rust-shrouded lump of metal that on closer examination resolved itself into an old car, an old Studebaker, the old 29 cent Studebaker—the only car on which I have ever turned a profit. The gas was worth more than the car, and that at a time when gasoline was 20 cents a gallon.

Sharing A Treasure

Amherst is a long way from Monomoy. Amherst is where a small group of us, all veterans, were attending the state university. We were only a few years older than the rest of the undergraduates, but most of us felt at least a generation older. I kept urging some of this group to come to the Cape to try for the fish that were particularly plentiful here in the fall of the year. They were all fresh water fishermen. I thought they needed some salt water experience to complete their education. I also wanted to share the treasures of Monomoy with my friends. One weekend, three of them accepted the invitation.

We arrived at the little island camp about 10 pm, and promptly turned in, but not before setting the alarm for 2 am—the time the tide turned on Schooner Bar, one of the best bars for intercepting the fall run of the big bass. The alarm did its thing, and we groggily rose to the challenge. Warm clothes, boots, fishpoles, a thermos of hot coffee, and we were ready for some night fishing.

The old beach car was roused to duty once again, and once again it came through, carrying us the mile or so out to the bar. It was a very dark night, though even on the darkest nights there is some light. It seemed we weren't the only ones who wanted to catch one of those migrating bass. Against the white of the surf we could just make out two shadowy figures by the water's edge and unfortunately they were right where I wanted to place my gang.

I explained to the crew that when the tide changed, the baitfish were swept over the bar and the big bass knew to take advantage of this confusion in the roiled waters. These wave-lashed waters were nothing to the bass with their strong bodies and broad tails, designed to let them move easily amid the surging waters. I described how the stripers would move into the shallow waters along the downtide side of the bars for the easy feeding. Then I placed my neophytes about 50 feet apart as close to the two ghostly strangers and the wave-washed bar as possible. I wished them luck and started to get my own gear ready.

Out of the darkness up to my left came a whoop loud enough to have been heard back in Amherst. What luck, somebody was already hooked up. There is no better way to start a fishing addiction than to catch a big fish on the very first trip. Whoever was doing the yelling was excited and letting the world know all about it. We all drifted up towards Jack, for it was this normally phlegmatic soul that was so energized. As we approached him in the black night, it looked as if he and one of the unknown shadowy figures were hugging and dancing around. Fishing is fun, no question about it, but this was the first time I'd ever seen two strangers hugging each other over fishing success. How big was this fish to elicit such fervent enthusiasm?

When the two of them could finally utter coherent words, the reason for the enthusiastic display was explained. It had nothing to do with fish- that was probably the last thing on their minds. These two men who happened to be standing next to each other on a 10-mile stretch of deserted beach had last seen each other in a foxhole on a rocky hillside in Korea. What quirk of happenstance put these two foxhole buddies on the same, all but deserted beach, at 2 am? We pondered this question the rest of the night, as we fished Schooner Bar into the dawn. They say happiness, like cold or heat, is invisible. Anyone from any walk of life looking at Jack and Carroll in the dawning morning, with the sun full on their faces, would have seen happiness. These two men, who had lived through dangerous times in an unforgiving land, had a bond that few share. They had never expected to see each other again. This most accidental meeting was as dramatic as it was unexpected. The light of a good friendship was once again burning brightly.

Winter Sailing

Monomoy plays host to the southward wending of big fish in the fall, the last hurrah before the cold grip of winter fastens its icy hand on the land. Seals and sea ducks also flee before the icy blasts, some to winter on the Cape. Monomoy plays host to these multitudes and displays a bleak beauty that only winter brings out.

December is a time when Pete and I decided we would do a little sailing in his old dory. Someone had donated a tender (half rotten) sail rig from a long deceased dory and we wanted to try it out. December was the month when Pete and I decided to go to the camp. It was college Christmas break, we could try out the "new" sail, check out the camp and get an infusion of Hospital Creek clams to last us until spring break.

The camp was five miles southwest of Stage Harbor, five miles of sailing—a time when I had my first experience with pure cold. We sailed from Stage Harbor in the 18-foot dory. The prevailing northwest wind filled the sail and pushed us along smartly. There is a certain joy in the semi-silence of sailing, the swoosh of the waves, the rustle of the wind in the sail. We reached the camp in good time and congratulated ourselves on an easy and uneventful sail. The food was unloaded and lugged over the dune to that snug camp, tucked down in its patch of beach plum bushes. It was time to settle in.

Settling in—in camp parlance, particularly in the winter— meant getting a fire going and fast. The old six-hole Glenwood was crammed with all the dry wood it would hold, and touched off. A Glenwood six holer is a remarkable stove. It heats well, it cooks well, and does so with a minimum of fuss. All one had to do was flip the bake/kindle lever to kindle, touch a match to the kindling, and the stove would do the rest. I've heard all manner of stories about the terrible time people have had trying to light wood stoves. They never met the old Glenwood. The only time the camp stove ever misbehaved was not really the stove's fault. A drying sneaker fell against the stovepipe and opened up a foot long hole in the side of it. Unbeknownst to us the stovepipe over the years had given up the ghost, had turned into a cylindrical column of rust. For a little while it was instructive to marvel at the smoke and flame roaring up by the hole, then we woke up to the fact that if all of the pipe was as tender as the piece that fell out, we were on the way to camp meltdown and we'd better do something about the situation. There is nothing like a foot or so of open flame in a tinder dry, wooden, beach camp to focus the mind.

On this cold December day, heat in the camp was a priority soon rectified. The next priority, taking advantage of the super low tide to get a mess of clams over in Hospital Creek—home of some of the best tasting clams in the world. The wind that had so smartly pushed us along in the dory was still blowing at a pretty good clip, and it was no longer helping us. It was congealing us as it scythed across the flats. However, clams will be clams. They had left their characteristic, telltale, dimples on the flats. With the freezing wind as a goad, we had a meal of steamers out of those flats in no time.

Coming back to the camp from a half mile trek, in boots through beach sand, into the teeth of a snarling, eye squinching, northwest half-gale, hands numb, nose dripping, chilled through to the bone was not a bit pleasant. But coming into the camp, and having its almost palpable heat flood over and engulf you, well that's one definition of bliss. It's a magnificent feeling to know that you have plenty of dry wood, plenty of clams ready to cook. All you have to do is slowly thaw out, a delicious process of the camp's heat incrementally driving out the cold of those bone chilling, arctic blasts. The excitement of the sailing trip, the frigid ordeal of the clam gathering, the early darkness, and our full stomachs combined with the 80 degree temperature of the camp acted as a mighty soporific of the most powerful kind. No sleeping pills are ever needed by the camp's people. With the meal over, the only noise heard was the roaring, probing wind, the distant, muted, rumble of surf on Schooner Bar, the slow, metallic ticking noise of the iron stove slowly cooling off, and the deep rumbling, snoring of relaxing bodies. A December day on Monomoy.

When we left the island the next day to head home, the wind hadn't let up a bit. It was still half a gale but it was now from the northeast, which put Stage Harbor five long miles upwind. Sailboats don't do upwind, sailing dories like upwind even less than sailboats. The dory went, oh how she went. She lay over on her side and scooted along. We made good time, moved along very well, but each time we came about (changed direction) the rents in the tattered, discolored sail opened a little wider slowing us more and more. We were on a nearly perpendicular course to our destination. We gained a little on each tack, enough to keep us going, but not enough to encourage us much.

During the ordeal, I remembered a lesson my grandfather

taught me about salt and ice when making ice cream. The ice cream mixture was cranked in a mixture of salt and ice. Grampa explained that salt is added to the ice because it lowers the temperature of liquid water.

We sailed back in just such a mixture of salt water and ice. Pete and I came to appreciate just how low the temperature of this salt ice could be. Each tack of the old dory was accompanied by sheets of salt spray coming over the windward rail. Five miles upwind became at least 10 miles of tacking (it seemed like a hundred miles). Every inch of that 10 miles an introduction to more of that frigid salt water. By the time we traveled the interminable distance back to Mitchell River, we both felt we had been through more water than some of the fish in Nantucket Sound. The sail had a layer of ice all over its lower edges, each slat of the sail sent a spray of salt ice over our numb bodies. The boom looked like a giant comb with icicles every few inches. In retrospect, of course, we should have stayed on the island and waited for a more favorable wind, or at the very least, less wind, at the time we thought getting back to college the most important goal, so we pushed on past prudence. By the time we got back to the car, we must have looked pretty grim. The dory was ice sheathed, the dories sail was ice sheathed, our clothes were ice sheathed. We sailed her in though, got her unrigged, anchored, and tried to get in the car. That's when we first realized just how cold we really were. We couldn't get the car keys out of our pockets, try as we might. Our fingers were no longer connected to our brain. We really didn't feel all that cold but nothing worked except our legs, and I guess our brain was working a little too because when it eventually became obvious that nothing we could do would get us the keys, we stood in the middle of the road until someone came along. We figured whoever it was he probably wouldn't run us over. He didn't, instead he retrieved the keys, unlocked the car, started it for us and left it running with the heater turned to full. He left us shaking his head. We would liked to have been able to shake his hand.

It was a long, thawing, painful, ride back to Amherst, and quite a long time before we thought much about winter sailing again. Winter camp trips were walking trips for the next few years.

Most trips to this 10-mile long playground were not painful, they were not hurtful, they were just fun. September, early September is a time college-bound young people are getting ready for the year of hard work that they know lies ahead, switching from summer's manual labor to the mental labor looming ahead. We all wanted one more party before the last year of the college grind began. The little camp on Monomoy was the site of just such a party one glorious early September day.

We four—Pete and his date, me and mine—had been down to the Powder Hole at the very tip of the beach to dig a mess of clams. It was a high tide dig. One normally digs clams at low tide, but we had some serious time constraints. It was high tide digging or no digging for our last clam meal for some time. It was a flat calm day. The mosquitoes were unmerciful, relentless and persistent—so much so that our snorkeling masks soon had the itching bugs flying around inside. It was a frustrating situation; you can't slap a mosquito in your face mask. You're lucky if you don't inhale it. It was frustrating but it didn't slow our harvest. Digging underwater, we managed to get enough clams for the evening's bacchanal. As we came out of the water a couple of young men, strangers our age, came over the dunes. They had been watching us, wondering what we were doing. They knew you couldn't dig clams at high tide. They, too, were facing a college year and were spending their last weekend camping on the sun-drenched dunes of Monomoy. This after spending a summer canoe camping well up in the wilds of Canada. We invited them back to the camp to share the repast. It was nearly dark when we arrived at the camp. In no time the old stove was fired, the clams kettled, and the stories began to fly. These were pretty interesting guys. They had had a great summer mostly on their own, miles from civilization. We shared stories, swapped recipes, quahog chowder for sour dough bread. It didn't seem very long before the clams boiled over the requisite three times and we were able to introduce our guests to steamed clams a la Monomoy—washed in their own broth and drenched with butter. In those halcyon days, we were all going to live forever. Butter? Lay it on. The meal was a huge success; the camp was hot, the light from the old kerosene lamps yielded a soft yellow glow, and our stomachs were pleasantly full. The gauge that measured pleasure also read *full*. The delightful experience of meeting really nice people and exploring their worlds carried the evening on into the night. We had no conception of time. The stories rolled on, the hours flew happily by, we were in a cocoon of happiness in that tiny hot camp. Eventually, overriding our inspired talking we noticed, felt rather, a rumbling noise, a rumbling feeling. This was something new, but what in God's name was it? We had been witness to many strange things on the island, but never any such rumbling as this. It was beyond the ken of our experiences. Whatever it was, it got slowly louder, pots and pans on the stove were noisily vibrating and rattling. What was going on. Whatever it was, we were beginning to vibrate and rattle. Whatever it was, was outside the camp. For the observers, we must have looked like ants leaving a collapsing anthill. Parked 50 feet above the snuggled down camp was a blimp with about six or eight guys looking down on us. The two huge motors were holding the aircraft steady against the light southwest wind and causing the rumbling noise. We were the only light, however dim, for five or six miles around. They had come down to investigate. They looked about our age. We tried to yell across the rumble to no avail. After a few fruitless attempts at communication they waved, we waved in return, and like the solid cloud they resembled, drifted away, taking their rumble with them.

This unusual break in the flow of conversation jarred us enough to realize it was late, about 3 am—three hours after we had promised to get the girls home. Maybe we'd best be getting our new-found friends back to their tents five miles down the beach and then get the girls home. About this time we noticed, well to the north, a set of headlights weaving and bobbing their way down the beach in our general direction, and idly wondered who would be driving the beach at this ungodly hour. Fisherman probably. The old beach car was sparked into life. We all piled in for the ride down that spectacular moonlit beach. It was an uneventful ride down the beach, if driving by the light of a full moon along the ocean's edge can be called uneventful, gloriously uneventful. As we were standing around exchanging addresses someone remarked that the headlights we had noticed from the camp were still doggedly coming on down the beach. As a matter of fact they seemed to be following our rather erratic tracks pretty closely. This was a real puzzle. There was little traffic on the beach anytime, rarely any at 3 am, and fishermen didn't come back here in the dunes. A casual mystery. We said our goodbyes, and promised to stay in touch. As we were pulling away the mystery car pulled up alongside. There were two men inside and in the reflection of their headlights, the puzzle pieces came together with a resounding flash of understanding and chagrin. We had promised to get the girls back by midnight, those two men were my irate father and Pam's apoplectic father. This glorious moonlit night held no beauty for them; they would much rather have been home in bed, they had to go to work in a few hours. For the four of us, going away to college suddenly became an attractive thought.

After a couple of years had passed, my Dad could finally chuckle a little about the experience. He related how at 1 am, one of the girls' father had called and understandably wanted to know where his daughter was. As my father was sound asleep at the time, and not privy to the whereabouts of me let alone my date, he had no idea in the world where the girl might be, other than probably somewhere on Monomoy. And it wasn't just any father calling, it was a cousin, family. Eventually the worried father prevailed on my dad to the point the two of them decided to see if they could find us, thinking that maybe we were in some kind of trouble. So for my dad, it was up out of the warm bed, get dressed, pick up the other father and head for Chatham five miles away. Then it was, drag the skiff down to the harbors edge, row across Stage Harbor, start the old Ford V-8, and drive miles down the beach in search of their wayward offspring. When they arrived at the camp where they fully expected us to be, all they found was, an open door, lit lanterns, a still warm stove, clam shells in profusion, and tire tracks heading down the beach. They figured we had to be where the tire tracks ended so they followed in a Monomoy version of hot pursuit to the "capture" at the tent site. They picked up the two girls for deliverance from durance vile, and headed back with vocal and vociferous imprecations. We decided that the better part of valor would be to spend the night at camp, come home the next day when upset fathers would be groggily at work. We were ready to spend a year at school far from home.

But these mild adventures were only the high spots, the everyday simple lifestyle lingers in the memory with just as much resonance—slipping over to Hospital Creek for a mess of clams for dinner, plucking of a bluefish or bass off Schooner Bar for the same purpose, or maybe picking a batch of blueberries in Wildcat Swamp. Figuring out the myriad of construction problems at no cost, these were all projects entailing discussion and planning, togetherness. Or maybe just doing nothing all day, lounging around talking about projects and never stirring enough ambition to move thought to action. And it all centered around the little camp. This building didn't amount to much. It would be disdained if it was in anyone's backyard, probably condemned, but by some alchemy, by being on that beach, at that time, it was transformed into a jewel beyond compare. The memories it engenders will always be of that special place and of that special time that will never again occur. And the memories will be treasured for that very reason.

In the mid-1980s the eroding beach was playing no favorites—the camp was standing still, the shore creeping ever closer and now what had happened to so many beach front buildings was about to happen to the little beach shanty.

Now (1997) 13 years later, I like to think that during one of that fall's raging easterlies, the camp gave a last wry chuckle as the ocean's battering waves changed it into interesting driftwood scattered along the shore—someone else's treasures that in the heat of day probably still had the faintest aroma of chicken.

In the short space of sixty years the little building came and left the island it graced. Actually the island left the camp. What a magnificent time, what a magnificent place that was for us. Sometimes, when I'm in a down mood, I go down into the basement and look at an old, worm-eaten, notched ships knee still half covered with candle wax. That notch fit around the bunkroom cornerpost and that ship's knee held the reading light, a candle, and some books. This is the only tangible link with the little camp that had sheltered something for its entire life. It is a fitting reminder of those times, like most of the rest of the material in the old place it too had been recycled and used again. Looking at the ancient shipbuilders art, at the wax drippings and that little notch, the memories jump to the forefront of my mind.

I have only to think back to the incredible good fortune that enabled me to be in the right place at the right time. To think back to a kind and generous uncle and all the people that have, with no thought of reward, helped along the way, to know I have been the most fortunate of men.

The camp site is now at least some hundred yards off shore. The omnipotent, heaving ocean covers the spot, but in my mind, when I "look" at the camp, it will always be snugged down in the hollow, the big sheltering beach plum bush that never bore, looming over the bunk room. It will be a bit foggy. A battered car, but a treasure nonetheless, probably a Model A, will be sitting nearby with tendrils of steam escaping from under the hood. Inside, something will be bubbling on the stove. I'll be leaning against the lookout tower looking down at the kerosene lantern's soft yellow glow streaming out of the windows in the mist laden air. The camp "looks" like a star down from the heavens, and I realize it was my shining star, and my bountiful earthbound heaven.◆

Epilogue

South Chatham today still guards the western flank of town; the same creeks and rivers flow, and the beaches are as beautiful. But there have been many changes. Houses have replaced the woods near West Meadow where I summered in a tent. Most of the dirt roads are gone, and the cranberry bogs are woefully overgrown. Even the weather seems to have moderated. Few winters now are cold enough to sheath the bogs and ponds for skating.

And while the beaches are about the same, they are hundreds of feet further north. The gentle embayments and marsh creeks have given way to a steadily eroding shoreline. With each decrease in the marsh a corresponding decrease in the shellfish populations follows. Not to paint too black a picture, though. The shellfish are still available if you look hard enough and know where to look. The Eel Pond River is still rife with clams, quahogs, and occasionally an oyster or scallop can be found. The shoal water off the old flake yard (between Forest Beach and the Pleasant Street beaches) seems to have a fair number of quahogs and this was a barren area in my childhood.

The increasing human presence has changed the face of the land. The freedoms we took for granted are often not possible anymore. All my life, the Cape's open spaces have been shrinking, and this is a worrisome fact. Luckily some far sighted people saw what was coming and created the Cape Cod National Seashore for all of us to enjoy. With the preservation of 28,000 acres, the Federal Government accomplished what none of us could do—hold the line on development.

There was some private heartbreak in the process, some in our immediate family as our ancestral lands were taken for the public good, but the overall feeling is that in the long run it is for the best. My grandchildren, their grandchildren and all the generations to follow will know parts of the Cape as I knew them. The same wild animals, the same wild birds, the same living resources will delight them as they delighted me. That makes me feel very comfortable.

Unlike the mainland, Monomoy is in constant rebirth. In the mid-1980s the ocean poked another hole through this barrier beach into Nantucket Sound. This occurred about halfway down the island, just north of Inward Point. It sounded the death knell for most of the camps that remained in this pristine environment. As this new inlet widened and stabilized, one camp after another, including my recycled chicken house, went through the minuet of demise:

First, the entombing of the camp by the encroaching beach, followed by a seeming respite — the unearthing of the camp on the seaward side of the beach dune. The view was magnificent but it was a final view, as the ocean continued its inexorable advance. Then the shingles were stripped off by the ocean's battering ways. A later storm started peeling off the boards themselves, then the structural timbers went. Soon the last vital support fell as well as the building itself. And at this point, the structure lost its identity. Now it was no longer a camp, just driftwood along the shore.

This was difficult for me to watch. I saw the camp entombed. I saw it coming out of the beach with the hungry surf licking at the shingles, and I didn't want to see any more.

Bird And Clam Factory

The peninsula I knew as a child is now three separate islands — Morris Island, North Monomoy, and South Monomoy. Morris Island and Monomoy separated from the mainland in 1938, and Monomoy separated from Morris Island in 1961.

Morris Island, now connected to the mainland by an earthen dike, is all developed — homes scattered all over the rolling hills, some with views to rival nation's best. *No Trespassing* signs blossom where once only the beach plum held sway.

Just south of Morris Island, the 1961 breakthrough separates this island from the first of the real beach. This thin strip of sand and its surrounding flats are home to thousands of shorebirds in the warmer months, and millions of clams year round. The grassy dunes shelter a myriad of the nesting birds of summer. This seemingly barren, almost sterile, stretch of white plays host to burgeoning life in colossal numbers—a two or three mile bird and clam factory now called North Monomoy.

The third and last of Monomoy's islands, South Monomoy, is the biggest. It is longer and wider than North Monomoy, five miles long and a half mile to a mile wide. It is also the only one of the three original bits of real estate that is actually making land. This strip of sand has a varied habitat, and near the Point itself it boasts two fairly sizable fresh water ponds. Hidden away in a beach plum patch are half a dozen ancient apple trees that on occasion still bear gigantic green fruit. A small herd of hungry deer roam the wetlands, muskrats tunnel the pond edges and make scarcely a dent in the dense stands of their favorite food—the cattail roots. One of the more unlikely inhabitants of this stretch of sand are color mutated (no stripes) garter snakes. They must find life around the pond edges easy, toads and insects in every size punctuate the white sands from spring until fall.

Here at the Point the beach is building. The forces of the tides keep whittling away the sands, but not as fast as the donations from the north keep depositing their loads. The result is a marked swing to the southwest. This finger of sand now seems to be reaching for Martha's Vineyard rather than its closest neighbor, Nantucket.

The Powder Hole, once Monomoy Point's harbor, is now just a vestige of its former self. It is almost completely cut off from tidal flow, only the highest tides keep the little harbor salt. Soon they too will cease to spill over the beach. The surrounding belt of beach grass is trapping the windblown sand and raising the dune level beyond the tides reach. Gradually, over time, this still deep little basin will change from today's salt pond to yet another fresh water pond ten miles at sea. I hope the name *Powder Hole* will still identify it.

The one camp left on the island is here at the harbor where once an entire village (Whitewash Village) ringed the water's edge. Dominating all, on the highest dune, was a Coast Guard station painted the traditional white with red roof—an easily visible landmark from sea even when the island itself was below the horizon. The long abandoned station was blown up by the government in an cataclysmic beach cleanup effort. All that now remains on that dune is a concrete pimple, the cistern that once supplied the station with water. The human presence at the Point is all but gone; that one old camp and a mile or so to the north, the Civil War era lighthouse still hold sway over those hauntingly beautiful dunes.

In terms of ownership the island has come full circle. In the time of the Native Americans, no one owned this strip of sand. William Nickerson's purchase in 1640 formalized land ownership; he owned Chatham including Monomoy. On the paternal side of my family, Levi Eldridge purchased about 500 acres of beach and meadow at Inward Point in 1869. The circle closed when the Federal Government took over the island in the late 1930s. Now, once again, all the inhabitants of the land own this lovely place.

The government's involvement with this island began in the late 1930s. As I understand the evolution of its ownership, it was first taken over as a flyway refuge, then immediately loaned to the Department of Defense as a training site for bombers. As soon as the war ended, the ownership reverted to the Department of Interior for use again as a flyway refuge. Some time later the designation changed to Wilderness Area, which it is today. This latest designation is apt and fitting for one of the last remaining wild areas extant on Cape Cod.

While the human presence has all but vanished from this island, the wildlife forms that have always called this place home have thrived. The largest animals (deer) of my time on the beach are still there, but they are no longer the biggest animals. The rare gray seal has taken over the role of biggest and are a year-round presence. The males run about 1500 pounds and are unlikely to be eclipsed anytime soon by anything larger. Where I considered myself lucky to see one harbor seal a winter, now hundreds if not thousands use Monomoy's welcoming beaches as a haul-out spot each winter.

The finfish we used to pursue are here. The striped bass are here seasonally and in far greater numbers than anything we ever saw. Stripers are common where we saw none. Big bass (the minimum legal size *was* 16 inches and is *now* 34 inches) are all females, and these fish are now being allowed to spawn a number of times before being taken by the fishermen. The federal government's management plan is working well. Bluefish are still raising the adrenaline level of anglers at Point Rip and all along the various shoals fringing the island. Their numbers seem to be happily confounding the scientists predictions of 40-year cycles of abundance and scarcity. We saw the first ones in 1949, Now in 1996 these aggressive fish are still there for the taking every summer. Those yellow eyed, sharp toothed fish fight with ferocity, taste very good and bring out the fishermen in droves.

The numerous new shoals attending the breakthroughs are garlanded with steamer clams, millions of clams. What's left of Hospital Creek still produces good clam crops, but the surrounding flats are richer in their shellfish bounty than they were when I was scratching the flats. For a brief period a bonanza of sea clams showed up near the delta of the Inward Point breakthrough. They were so thick you could hardly get a rake between them. This apparently was a one time event, unique and somewhat awe inspiring.

Bird populations have changed dramatically in the intervening 40 years. Gulls of all persuasions are nesting all over the beaches, again where we saw hardly a bird. These omnivorous birds follow man closely and benefit from our sloppy handling of waste, hence their surge in numbers. Terns numbers seem to be in decline, they have trouble fending off the hungry gulls hence their numbers are dropping.

Our burgeoning numbers doomed our way of life on Monomy. There were just plain too many of us to let the free and easy ways of my youth continue. Two or three of us on the dunes in our beach buggies did little harm. Nature could keep up with our depredations. Nature wouldn't stand a chance against today's hordes. That the Feds took over the island hurt us badly, the ache is still there, but like the much larger Outer Cape, the alternative of uncontrolled development was a much worse scenario. So we swallow hard and with a stiff upper lip allow as how this present situation with all its restrictions is in the end, the best solution.

Wib's Final Trip

My family all love Monomoy with a deep abiding passion. One beautiful summer day not too long ago I took my father on a one-way trip to the island. I talked to him all the way across the seven miles of Nantucket Sound, told him how nice the day was, told him I knew how much he appreciated the beauty and serenity of this very special place. I told him I knew how very much he loved being on the island of our ancestors. I told him I remembered the story he once told near the end of his life, how even if he couldn't walk, he would crawl, if I would only get him to the island. Like all of us, his love for this land went deep. This last trip with him, to spread his ashes, was done with mixed feelings — great sadness to be leaving him, great joy in knowing I had fulfilled his fervent oft-stated desire.

Where Monomoy goes so goes Wib. He is now part of the very fabric of the island. A major storm took his first camp, the Government took his second camp, but he is now on Monomoy to stay. His ashes are now a part of the landscape. May he enjoy those magnificent sunsets across the sound, may he savor the clams all around him, may he enjoy being near the still extant hearth that marks the site of his first camp on the island — that hearth that heard so much laughter, that saw so much contentment swirling around it, and saw so much driftwood go up the flue.

Being there will give him peace for all time, something we all crave.◆

About the Author

Dana Eldridge is a Cape Codder of many generations standing. His association with his beloved land encompasses a lifetime in and around the beaches and the salt water that permeate Cape Cod. Mr Eldridge writes a bi-weekly column for a local paper, *The Cape Codder*, on the natural world of this lovely peninsula.